Voices of Sanity
Reaching Out For Peace

Voices of Sanity
Reaching Out For Peace

Edited by

Kamla Bhasin
Smitu Kothari
Bindia Thapar

JAGORI

Lokayan

Rainbow

Voices of Sanity was first published in India in 2001 by
Lokayan, 13, Alipur Road, Delhi - 110054,
Jagori, C-54, South Extension, Part II, New Delhi - 110049 and
Rainbow Publishers, A-19, Sector 56, NOIDA, UP - 201301.

ISBN 81-86962-301-1 (Pb)

Set in AGaramond and Humanist by Vinay Aditya
and printed and bound by him at Systems Vision, New Delhi

Acknowledgements

There are many dangers in publishing a collection of responses to the horrific events of September 11 so soon after they happened. Yet, as we began to receive messages and streams of consciousness and articles and poems and reports of peace vigils and marches that reflected and illuminated our own feelings, we were struck by the depth and range of expression. Bombarded by the aggressiveness of dominant voices, we felt it was a political act to put other voices - voices of sanity - together.

Once word got out that we were putting this collection together and wanted to release it a month after the tragedy, we were overwhelmed by what friends around the world began to send us. We are particularly grateful to Harsh Kapoor, CF John, Sheba Chhachhi, Arturo Escobar, Karen McGuinness, Dhruva Narayan, Ritu Menon, Tahira Thapar, Syeda Hameed, Paul Gonsalves, Karamat Ali, Mary Kaldor, Mishka Zaman, Sabine Hammer, Wendy Harcourt, Praful Bidwai and so many others who sent us material. A special word of gratitide for Juhi Jain who tirelessly facilitated the processing and transfer of all this material between computers around the world.

Our colleagues at Jagori and Lokayan bore our hassled states for over two weeks. We celebrate their support and are grateful to Hemlata Shankar of Orient Longman, Delhi, and Radhika Menon of Tulika Books, Chennai for permission to use visual material originally created for their publications, and to Vinay Aditya for responding so spontaneously to our request to produce this book within a record ten days.

We dedicate this to the victims of violence everywhere and to the indomitable urge for justice, dignity and peace.

Peace activists lighting candles at Wagah, August 14-15, 2001.
Photograph by Sheba Chhachhi

Voices

Voices of Sanity

On September 19, 300 of us gathered together and sat in concentric circles at the India Gate in Delhi as twilight gradually descended on the horizon. We lit candles and sat in a vigil – a powerful ring of solidarity. As we reached out, held hands, hugged old friends and looked into the eyes of those we did not know, we were sharing a commonly felt sense of frustration and anger at how easily those who claim to be our political leaders can talk of war, of how easily our Defence and External Affairs minister, Jaswant Singh, could speak of a "concert of democracies" that would collaborate to defend "civilisation".

As the sun was setting and the candles lit forth our concerned faces, we pledged to come together – across political persuasion and institution, across age and class. A few days later, representatives of a very wide cross-section of organisations marched from the Red Fort to Ferozshah Kotla grounds through some of Delhi's busiest streets. This was one of the very few times since 1984, when thousands of Sikhs were massacred on the streets of Delhi and elsewhere in the country, that so many of us representing such a diverse range of groups and coalitions and movements came together.

The violent attacks on September 11 have extinguished a slice of humanity – not just in New York and Washington, but around the world. Even though some of us are thousands of miles away, we share the fear and anguish that such horrific acts create and would like to take this opportunity to offer our deepest sense of solidarity for all those who have lost links in their families and communities.

September 11 has also changed the definition of what constitutes security. It is no longer the debate between national security and people's security. Now, and for years to come, it will be the backlash, in the name of "dealing with terrorism", against individuals and countries. The backlash will be justified in the name of security. There will even be efforts to delegitimise democratic struggles that challenge the dominant ethos – for instance, the growing mobilisations against a thoroughly undemocratic and unjust process of economic globalisation will be labelled as mobilisations that threaten the politically dominant effort to build a "secure" and "civilised" world.

For most of the two weeks since the attacks, the media, increasingly controlled by corporate monopolies in India and the West have been presenting only one side of the interventions needed in the aftermath of the attacks on the World Trade Centre and the Pentagon – interventions that would increase hatred and intolerance, reduce freedoms and further shrink democratic space.

There is another set of voices - reflective, incisive, historically contextualised, committed to restraint, tolerance, and peace. This booklet presents some of these voices - voices, we believe, that mirror a much wider and deeper sensibility, representing a majority of the human race. It is this majority that has been victimised by so many hegemonies, processes of domination and exclusion - the hegemony of militarisation, of centuries of conquest and domination, of fundamentalist and intolerant regimes, of patriarchy in all its manifestations, of repression that is directly and indirectly supported by the leaders of the most powerful nations in the world, of economic globalisation that socially, culturally and economically threatens most of the planet, of development patterns that fatten the rich and enfeeble the poor, that increasingly treat all life as a commodity amenable to ruthless exploitation and manipulation. More and more people, and nations, have lost even basic control over their lives. On a massive scale, their livelihoods, systems of meaning and of identity have been threatened and even destroyed.

The victims of New York and Washington are joined by millions of other victims – millions who have lost their lives and livelihoods because of the caste and class that they were born into, because of the forests and lands and water systems that they lived with that have been, often brutally, alienated from them, who have had their cultures and communities and the bones of their ancestors submerged under development projects, who have perished or experience terror because of the violence inside families. These violence's and their inter-relationship have also to be understood as we probe deeper into the root causes of the violence of September 11. We have marched with many of their victims, stood by their side as they demanded dignity and justice – not the "infinite justice" of the American state or the "justice" of extremists but economic justice, social justice, ecological justice, justice sought by the inner core of individuals and peoples that stand violated at this moment of truth for humanity as a whole.

The voices gathered in this compilation here reflect this urge – an urge that might express itself in the lighting of a candle at a peace vigil, in peace marches, at a silent demonstration with a placard, "No violence, not now, not ever!" The urge also expresses itself in the probing analysis that lays bare the machinations of those in power and the immorality of their aggressive responses as well as the myriad ways in which the popular mind is sought to be manipulated. We also see the urge in the resistance in so many spheres to oppression and discrimination, in the struggles to define lifestyles that respect the limits of the planet, in the organising of local and regional and global collective responses, in the dreams and visions of a family, a neighbourhood, a community and a world that is free of the merchants of economic and cultural homogenisation and of death.

On September 19, during the vigil at India Gate, a call went out to friends to organise peace vigils across the country and the world on October 2, Gandhi's birth anniversary. This Global Peace Vigil generated an overwhelming response. We have received news that vigils were held in atleast 40 countries and in cities and villages all over the country. Those who participated in these vigils, and the voices in this compilation, reflect the ever-widening impulse that could awaken massive mobilisations for a different kind of justice, a different kind of freedom, and a truly different kind of shared world. On this birthday of Gandhi, we solemnise here these voices of sanity.

Smitu Kothari
Kamla Bhasin
Bindia Thapar

October 2, 2001

no
more
silence

About War and Violence

Words by Kamla Bhasin, illustration by Bindia Thapar

The Theatre of Good and Evil

Eduardo Galeano

In the struggle of Good against Evil, it's always the people who get killed. The terrorists killed workers of 50 countries in NYC and DC, in the name of Good against Evil. And in the name of Good against Evil President Bush has promised vengeance: "We will eliminate Evil from the world", he announced.

Eliminate Evil? What would Good be without Evil? It's not just religious fanatics who need enemies to justify their insanity. The arms industry and the gigantic war machine of the US also needs enemies to justify its existence. Good and evil, evil and good: the actors change masks, the heroes become monsters and the monsters heroes, in accord with the demands of the theatre's playwrights.

This is nothing new. The German scientist Werner von Braun was evil when he invented the V-2 bombers that Hitler used against London, but became good when he used his talents in the service of the US. Stalin was good during World War Two and evil afterwards, when he became the leader of the Evil Empire. In the cold war years John Steinbeck wrote: "Maybe the whole world needs Russians. I suppose that even in Russia they need Russians. Maybe Russia's Russians are called Americans." Even the Russians became good afterwards. Today, Putin can add his voice to say: "Evil must be punished."

Saddam Hussein was good, and so were the chemical weapons he used against the Iranians and the Kurds. Afterwards, he became evil. They were calling him Satan Hussein when the US finished up their invasion of Panama to invade Iraq because Iraq invaded Kuwait. Father Bush that particular war against Evil upon himself. With the humanitarian and compassionate spirit that characterizes his family, he killed more than 100 000 Iraqis, the vast majority of them civilians.

Satan Hussein stayed where he was, but this number one enemy of humanity had to step aside and accept becoming number two enemy of humanity. The bane of the world is now called Osama bin Laden. The CIA taught him everything he knows about terrorism: bin Laden, loved and armed by the US government, was one of the principal 'freedom fighters' against Communism in Afghanistan. Father Bush occupied the Vice Presidency when President Reagan called these heroes 'the moral equivalents of the Founding Fathers.' Hollywood agreed. They filmed Rambo 3: Afghani Muslims were the good guys. Now, 13 years later, in the time of Son Bush, they are the worst of the bad guys.

Henry Kissinger was one of the first to react to the recent tragedy. "Those who provide support, financing, and inspiration to terrorists are as guilty as the terrorists themselves," he intoned, words that Son Bush would repeat hours later.

If that's how it is, the urgent need right now is to bomb Kissinger. He is guilty of many more crimes than bin Laden or any terrorist in the world. And in many more countries. He provided 'support, financing, and inspiration" to state terror in Indonesia, Cambodia, Iran, South Africa, Bangladesh, and all the South American countries that suffered the dirty war of Plan Condor.

On September 11 1973, exactly 28 years before the fires of last week, the Presidential Palace in Chile was stormed. Kissinger had written the epitaph of Allende and Chilean democracy long before when he commented on the results of the elections: "I don't see why we have to stand by and watch a country go communist because of the irresponsibility of its own people."

A contempt for the people is one of many things shared by state and private terror. For example, the ETA, an organization that kills people in the name of independence in Basque Country, says through one of its spokespeople: 'Rights have nothing to do with majorities or minorities.' There is much common ground between low- and high-tech terrorism, between the terrorism of religious fanatics and that of market fanatics, that of the hopeless and that of the powerful, that of the psychopath on the loose and that of the cold-blooded uniformed professional. They all share the disrespect for human life: the killers of the 5500 citizens under the Twin Towers that fell like castles of dry sand– and the killers of 200 000 Guatemalans, the majority of whom were indigenous, exterminated without television or the newspapers of the world paying any attention. Those Guatemalans were not sacrificed by any Muslim fanatic, but by terrorist squads who received 'support, financing, and inspiration' from successive US governments.

All these worshipers of death are in agreement as well on the need to reduce social, cultural, and national differences to military terms. In the name of Good against Evil, in the name of the One Truth, they resolve everything by killing first and asking questions later. And by this method, they strengthen the enemy they fight. It was the atrocities of the Sendero Luminoso that gave President Fujimori the popular support he sought to unleash a regime of terror and sell Peru for the price of a banana. It was the atrocities of the US in the Middle East that prepared the ground for the holy war of terrorism of Allah.

Although the leader of the Civilized World is pushing a new Crusade, Allah is innocent of the crimes committed in his name. At the end of the day, God did not order the Holocaust against the followers of Jehovah, nor did Jehovah order the massacres of Sabrah and Shatila or the expulsion of Palestinians from their land. Aren't Allah, God and Jehovah are, after all, three names for the same divinity?

A tragedy of errors: nobody knows any more who is who. The smoke of the explosions forms part of the much larger curtain of smoke that prevents all of us from seeing clearly. From revenge to revenge, terrorism obliges us to walk to our graves. I saw a photo, recently published, of graffiti on a wall in NYC: "An eye for an eye makes the whole world blind." The spiral of violence creates violence and also confusion: pain, fear, intolerance, hatred, insanity. In Porto Allegre, at the beginning of this year, Ahmed Ben Bella warned: 'This system, that has already made mad cows, is making mad people too." And these mad people, mad from hate, act as the power that created them.

A three-year-old child, named Luca, told me: "The world doesn't know where its house is." He was looking at a map. He could have been looking at a reporter.

Eduardo Galeano is one of Latin America's finest writers.

If we fail to speak up today
Deadly silence we will earn

Every home will be on fire
Every dwelling we'll see burn

From beyond the silence then
A cry of anguish will return

There's no one here
No one at all

No one.

Original Poem in Urdu by Sahir Ludhiyanwi. English translation by Kamla Bhasin. Illustration by Rajasthan Kisan Sanghatana.

Thoughts

Suheir Hammad

I.

there have been no words.
i have not written one word.
no poetry in the ashes south of canal street.
no prose in the refrigerated trucks driving debris and dna.
not one word.

today is a week, and seven is of heavens, gods, science.
evident out my kitchen window is an abstract reality.
sky where once was steel.
smoke where once was flesh.
fire in the city air and i feared for my sister's life in a way
never before. and then, and now, i fear for the rest of us.

first, please god, let it be a mistake, the pilot's heart failed,
the plane's engine died.
then please god, let it be a nightmare, wake me now.
please god, after the second plane, please, don't let
it be anyone
who looks like my brothers.

i do not know how bad a life has to break in order to kill.
i have never been so hungry that i willed hunger
i have never been so angry as to want to control a gun
over a pen.
not really.

even as a woman, as a palestinian, as a broken human being.
never this broken.

more than ever, i believe there is no difference.
the most privileged nation, most americans do not know the difference
between indians, afghanis, syrians, muslims, sikhs, hindus.
more than ever, there is no difference.

2.

thank you korea for kimchi and bibim bob, and corn tea and the genteel smiles of the wait staff at wonjo - smiles never revealing
the heat of the food or how tired they must be working long midtown shifts. thank you korea, for the belly craving that brought me into the city late the night before and diverted my daily train ride into the world trade centre.

there are plenty of thank yous in ny right now thank you for my lazy procrastinating late ass. thank you to the germs that had me call in sick. thank you, my attitude, you had me fired the week before. thank you for the train that never came, the rude nyer who stole my cab going downtown. thank you for the sense my mama gave me to run. thank you for my legs, my eyes, my life.

3.

the dead are called lost and their families hold up shaky printouts in front of us through screens smoked up.
we are looking for iris, mother of three. please call with any information. we are searching for priti, last seen on the 103rd floor. she was talking to her husband on the phone and the line went. please help us find george, also known as adel. his family is waiting for him with his favorite meal. i am looking for my son, who was delivering coffee. i am looking for my sister girl, she started her job on monday.

i am looking for peace. i am looking for mercy. i am looking for evidence of compassion. any evidence of life. i am looking for life.

4.

ricardo on the radio said in his accent thick as yuca, "i will feel so much better when the first bombs drop over there. and my friends feel the same way."

on my block, a woman was crying in a car parked and stranded in hurt. i offered comfort, extended a hand she did not see before she said, "we're gonna burn them so bad, i swear, so bad." my hand went to my head and my head went to the numbers within it of the dead iraqi children, the dead in nicaragua. the dead in rwanda who had to vie with fake sport wrestling for america's attention.

yet when people sent emails saying, this was bound to happen, lets not forget u.s. transgressions, for half a second i felt resentful. hold up with that, cause i live here, these are my friends and fam, and it could have been me in those buildings, and we're not bad people, do not support america's bullying. can i just have a half second to feel bad?

if i can find through this exhaust people who were left behind to mourn and to resist mass murder, i might be alright. thank you to the woman who saw me brinking my cool and blinking back tears. she opened her arms before she asked "do you want a hug?" a big white woman, and her embrace was the kind only people with the warmth of flesh can offer. i wasn't about to say no to any comfort. "my brother's in the navy," i said. "and we're arabs". "wow, you got double trouble." word.

5.
one more person ask me if i knew the hijackers.
one more motherfucker ask me what navy my brother is in.
one more person assume no arabs or muslims were killed.
one more person assume they know me, or that i represent a people. or that a people represent an evil. or that evil is as simple as a flag and words on a page.

we did not vilify all white men when mcveigh bombed oklahoma. america did not give out his family's addresses or where he went to church. or blame the bible or pat robertson. and when the networks air footage of palestinians dancing in the street, there is no apology that these images are over a decade old. that hungry children are bribed with sweets that turn their teeth brown. that correspondents edit images. that archives are there to facilitate lazy and inaccurate journalism.

and when we talk about holy books and hooded men and
death, why do we never mention the kkk?
if there are any people on earth who understand how new
york is feeling right now, they are in the west bank and
the gaza strip.

6.

today it is ten days. last night bush waged war on a man
once openly funded by the cia. i do not know who is responsible, read too many books, know too many people to
believe what i am told. i don't give a fuck about bin laden. his
vision of the world does not include me or those i love. and
petitions have been going around for years trying to get u.s.
sponsored taliban out of power. shit is complicated and i
don't know what to think. but i know for sure who will pay.

in the world, it will be women, mostly coloured and poor.
women will have to bury children, and support themselves
through grief. "either you are with us, or with the terrorists"
– meaning keep your people under control and your resistance censored. meaning we got the loot and the nukes.

in america, it will be those amongst us who refuse blanket
attacks on the shivering. those of us who work toward social
justice, in support of civil liberties, in opposition to hateful
foreign policies.

i have never felt less american and more new yorker –
particularly brooklyn than these past days. the stars and
stripes on all these cars and apartment windows represent
the dead as citizens first – not family members, not lovers.

i feel like my skin is real thin, and that my eyes are only
going to get darker. the future holds little light.

my baby brother is a man now, and on alert, and praying five
times a day that the orders he will take in a few days time
are righteous and will not weigh his soul down from the
afterlife he deserves. both my brothers – my heart stops
when i try to pray – not a beat to disturb my fear. one a
rock god, the other a sergeant, and both palestinian, practis-
ing muslim, gentle men. both born in brooklyn and their faces

are of the archetypical arab men. all eyelashes and nose and beautiful colour and stubborn hair.

what will their lives be like now?

over there is over here

7.

all day, across the river, the smell of burning rubber and limbs floats through. the sirens have stopped now. the advertisers are back on the air. the rescue workers are traumatised. the skyline is brought back to human size. no longer taunting the gods with its height.

i have not cried at all while writing this. i cried when i saw those buildings collapse on themselves like a broken heart. i have never owned pain that needs to spread like that. and i cry daily that my brothers return to our mother safe and whole.

there is no poetry in this. there are causes and effects. there are symbols and ideologies. mad conspiracy here, and information we will never know. there is death here and there are promises of more. there is life here. anyone reading this is breathing, maybe hurting but breathing for sure. and if there is any light to come it will shine from the eyes of those who look for peace and justice after the rubble and rhetoric are cleared and the phoenix has risen.

affirm life.

affirm life.

we got to carry each other now.

you are with life or against it.

affirm life.

Suheir Hammad is the author of Born Palestinian, Born Black. *Her column,* Psalm 26:7, in Stress, *is the longest running column written by a woman in an American music magazine.*

Illustration by C F John

Ghosts and Echoes

Robin Morgan

I'll focus on New York–my firsthand experience–but this doesn't mean any less anguish for the victims of the Washington or Pennsylvania calamities. Today was Day 8. Incredibly, a week has passed. Abnormal normalcy has settled in. Our usually contentious mayor (previously bad news for New Yorkers of colour and for artists) has risen to this moment with efficiency, compassion, real leadership. The city is alive and dynamic. Below 14th Street, traffic is flowing again, mail is being delivered, newspapers are back. But very early this morning I walked east, then south almost to the tip of Manhattan Island. The 16-acre site itself is closed off, of course, as is a perimeter surrounding it controlled by the National Guard, used as a command post and staging area for rescue workers. Still, one is able to approach nearer to the area than was possible last weekend, since the law-court district and parts of the financial district are now open and (shakily) working. The closer one gets the more one sees–and smells–what no TV report, and very few print reports, have communicated. I find myself giving way to tears again and again, even as I write this.

If the first sights of last Tuesday seemed bizarrely like a George Lucas special-effects movie, now the directorial eye has changed: it's the grim lens of Agnes Varda, juxtaposed with images so surreal they could have been framed by Bunuel or Kurosawa.

This was a bright, cloudless, early autumnal day. But as one draws near the site, the area looms out of a dense haze: one enters an atmosphere of dust, concrete powder, and plumes of smoke from fires still raging deep beneath the rubble (an estimated 2 million cubic yards of debris). Along lower 2nd Avenue, 10 refrigerator tractor-trailer trucks are parked, waiting; if you stand there a while, an NYC Medical Examiner van arrives–with a sagging body bag. Thick white ash, shards of broken glass, pebbles, and chunks of concrete cover street after street of parked cars for blocks outside the perimeter. Handprints on car windows and doors- handprints sliding downward–have been left like frantic graffiti. Sometimes there are messages finger-written in the ash: "U R Alive." You can look into closed shops, many with cracked or broken windows, and peer into another dimension: a wall-clock stopped at 9:10, restaurant tables meticulously set but now covered with two inches of ash, grocery shelves stacked with cans and produce bins piled high with apples and melons–all now powdered chalk-white. A moonscape of plenty. People walk unsteadily along these streets, wearing nosemasks against the still particle-full air, the stench of burning wire and plastic, erupted sewage; the smell of death, of decomposing flesh.

Probably your TV coverage shows the chain-link fences aflutter with yellow ribbons, the makeshift shrines of candles, flowers, scribbled notes of mourning or of praise for the rescue workers that have sprung up everywhere–especially in front of firehouses, police stations, hospitals. What TV doesn't show you is that near Ground Zero the streets for blocks around are still, a week later, adrift in bits of paper–singed, torn, sodden pages: stock reports, trading print-outs, shreds of appointment calendars, half of a "To-Do" list. What TV doesn't show you are scores of tiny charred corpses now swept into the gutters. Sparrows. Finches. They fly higher than pigeons, so they would have exploded outward, caught mid-air in a rush of flame, wings on fire as they fell. Who could have imagined it: the birds were burning.

From a distance, you can see the lattices of one of the Towers, its skeletal bones the sole remains, eerily beautiful in asymmetry, as if a new work of abstract art had been erected in a public space. Elsewhere, you see the transformation of institutions: The New School and New York University are missing persons' centres. A movie house is now a rest shelter, a Burger King a first-aid centre, a Brooks Brothers?? clothing store a body parts morgue, a record shop a haven for stranded animals. Libraries are counselling centres. Ice rinks are morgues. A bank is now a supply depot: in the first four days, it distributed 11,000 respirators and 25,000 pairs of protective gloves and suits. Nearby, a mobile medical unit housed in a Macdonald's has administered 70,000 tetanus shots. The brain tries to process the numbers: "only" 50,000 tons of debris had been cleared by yesterday, out of 1.2 million tons. The medical examiner's office has readied up to 20,000 DNA tests for unidentifiable cadaver parts. At all times, night and day, a minimum of 1000 people live and work on the site.

Such numbers daze the mind. It's the details–fragile, individual– that melt numbness into grief. An anklet with "Joyleen" engraved on it–found on an ankle. Just that: an ankle. A pair of hands–one brown, one white–clasped together. Just that. No wrists. A burly welder who drove from Ohio to help, saying softly, "We're working in a cemetery. I'm standing in–not on, in–a graveyard." Each lamppost, storefront, scaffolding, mailbox, is plastered with home-made photocopied posters, a racial/ethnic rainbow of faces and names: death the great leveller, not only of the financial CEOs–their images usually formal, white, male, older, with suit-and-tie–but the mailroom workers, receptionists, waiters. You pass enough of the MISSING posters and the faces, names, descriptions become familiar. The Albanian window-cleaner guy with the bushy eyebrows. The teenage Mexican dishwasher who had an American flag tattoo. The janitor's assistant who'd emigrated from Ethiopia. The Italian-American grandfather who was a doughnut-cart tender. The 23-year-old Chinese American junior pastry chef at the Windows on the World restaurant who'd gone in early that day so she could prep a business breakfast for 500. The fire-fighter who'd posed jauntily wearing his green shamrock necktie. The dapper African-American mid-level manager with a small gold ring in his ear who handled "minority affairs" for one of the companies. The middle-aged secretary laughing up at the camera from her wheelchair. The maintenance worker with a Polish name, holding his new-born baby. Most of the faces are smiling; most of the shots are family photos; many are recent wedding pictures. . . .

I have little national patriotism, but I do have a passion for New York, partly for our gritty, secular energy of endurance, and because the world does come here: 80 countries had offices in the Twin Towers; 62 countries lost citizens in the catastrophe; an estimated 300 of our British cousins died, either in the planes or the buildings. My personal comfort is found not in ceremonies or prayer services but in watching the plain, truly heroic (a word usually misused) work of ordinary New Yorkers we take for granted every day, who have risen to this moment unpretentiously, too busy even to notice they're expressing the splendour of the human spirit: fire-fighters, medical aides, nurses, ER doctors, police officers, sanitation workers, construction-workers, ambulance drivers, structural engineers, crane operators, rescue workers, tunnel rats. . . . Meanwhile, across the US, the rhetoric of retaliation is in full-throated roar. Flag sales are up. Gun sales are up. Some radio stations have banned playing John Lennon's song, "Imagine." Despite appeals from all officials (even Bush), mosques are being attacked, firebombed; Arab Americans are hiding their children indoors; two murders in Arizona have already been categorised as hate crimes–one victim a Lebanese-American man and one a Sikh man who died merely for wearing a turban. (Need I say that there were not nation-wide attacks against white Christian males after Timothy McVeigh was apprehended for the Oklahoma City bombing?)

Last Thursday, right-wing televangelists Jerry Falwell and Pat Robertson (our home-grown American Taliban leaders) appeared on Robertson's TV show "The 700 Club," where Falwell blamed "the pagans, and the abortionists, and the feminists and the gays and lesbians... the American Civil Liberties Union, People for the American Way" and groups "who have tried to secularise America" for what occurred in New York. Robertson replied, "I totally concur." After even the Bush White House called the remarks "inappropriate," Falwell apologised (though he did not take back his sentiments); Robertson hasn't even apologised. (The program is carried by the Fox Family Channel, recently purchased by the Walt Disney Company–in case you'd like to register a protest.)

The sirens have lessened. But the drums have started. Funeral drums. War drums. A State of Emergency, with a call-up of 50,000 reservists to active duty. The Justice Department is seeking increased authority for wider surveillance, broader detention powers, wiretapping of persons (not, as previously, just phone numbers), and stringent press restrictions on military reporting.

And the petitions have begun. For justice but not vengeance. For a reasoned response but against escalating retaliatory violence. For vigilance about civil liberties. For the rights of innocent Muslim Americans. For "bombing"Afghanistan with food and medical parcels, NOT firepower. There will be the expectable peace marches, vigils, rallies. . . . One member of the House of Representatives–Barbara Lee, Democrat of California, an African American woman–lodged the sole vote in both houses of Congress against giving Bush broadened powers for a war response, saying she didn't believe a massive military campaign would stop terrorism. (She could use letters of support: email her, if you wish, at barbara.lee@mail.house.gov)

Those of us who have access to the media have been trying to get a different voice out. But ours are complex messages with long-term solutions–and this is a moment when people yearn for simplicity and short-term, facile answers.

Still, I urge all of you to write letters to the editors of newspapers, call in to talk radio shows, and, for those of you who have media access–as activists, community leaders, elected or appointed officials, academic experts, whatever–to do as many interviews and TV programs as you can. Use the tool of the Internet. Talk about the root causes of terrorism, about the need to diminish this daily climate of patriarchal violence surrounding us in its state-sanctioned normalcy; the need to recognise people's despair over ever being heard short of committing such dramatic, murderous acts; the need to address a desperation that becomes chronic after generations of suffering; the need to arouse that most subversive of emotions–empathy–for "the other"; the need to eliminate hideous economic and political injustices, to reject all tribal/ethnic hatreds and fears, to repudiate religious fundamentalisms of every kind. Especially talk about the need to understand that we must expose the mystique of violence, separate it from how we conceive of excitement, eroticism, and "manhood"; the need to comprehend that violence differs in degree but is related in kind, that it thrives along a spectrum, as do its effects–from the battered child and raped woman who live in fear to an entire populace living in fear.

Meanwhile, we cry and cry and cry. I don't even know who my tears are for anymore, because I keep seeing ghosts, I keep hearing echoes.

The world's sympathy moves me deeply. Yet I hear echoes dying into silence: the world averting its attention from Rwanda's screams . . . Ground Zero is a huge mass grave. And I think: Bosnia. Uganda.

More than 6300 people are missing and presumed dead (not even counting the Washington and Pennsylvania deaths). The TV anchors choke up: civilians, they say, my god, civilians. And I see ghosts. Hiroshima. Nagasaki. Dresden. Vietnam.

I watch the mask-covered mouths and noses on the street turn into the faces of Tokyo citizens who wear such masks every day against toxic pollution. I watch the scared eyes become the fearful eyes of women forced to wear the hijab or chodor or burka against their will . . .

I stare at the missing posters' photos and think of the Mothers of the Disappeared, circling the plazas in Argentina. And I see the ghosts of other faces. In photographs on the walls of Holocaust museums. In newspaper clippings from Haiti. In chronicles from Cambodia . . . I worry for people who've lost their homes near the site, though I see how superbly social-service agencies are trying to meet their immediate and longer-term needs. But I see ghosts: the perpetually homeless who sleep on city streets, whose needs are never addressed. . . .

I watch normally unflappable New Yorkers flinch at loud noises, parents panic when their kids are late from school. And I see my Israeli feminist friends like Yvonne, who've lived with this dread for decades and still (even yesterday) stubbornly issue petitions insisting on peace. . . .

I watch sophisticates sob openly in the street, people who've lost workplaces, who don't know where their next paycheque will come from, who fear a contaminated water or food supply, who are afraid for their sons in the army, who are unnerved by security checkpoints, who are in mourning, who are wounded, who feel humiliated, outraged. And I see my friends like Zuhira in the refugee camps of Gaza or West Bank, Palestinian women who have lived in precisely that same emotional condition—for four generations.

Last weekend, many Manhattanites left town to visit concerned families, try to normalise, get away for a break. As they streamed out of the city, I saw ghosts of other travellers: hundreds of thousands of Afghan refugees streaming toward their country's borders in what is to them habitual terror, trying to escape a drought-sucked country so war-devastated there's nothing left to bomb, a country with 50,000 disabled orphans and two million widows whose sole livelihood is begging; where the life expectancy of men is 42 and women 40; where women hunch in secret whispering lessons to girl children forbidden to go to school, women who risk death by beheading–for teaching a child to read.

The ghosts stretch out their hands. Now you know, they weep, gesturing at the carefree, insulated, indifferent, golden innocence that was my country's safety, arrogance, and pride. Why should it take such horror to make you see? the echoes sigh, Oh please do you finally see?

This is calamity. And opportunity. The United States–what so many of you call America–could choose now to begin to understand the world. And join it. Or not.

For now my window still displays no flag, my lapel sports no red-white-and-blue ribbon. Instead, I weep for a city and a world. Instead, I cling to a different loyalty, affirming my un-flag, my un-anthem, my un-prayer–the defiant un-pledge of a madwoman who also had mere words as hourly tools in a time of ignorance and carnage, Virginia Woolf: "As a woman I have no country. As a woman I want no country. As a woman my country is the whole world."

If this is treason, may I be worthy of it.

In mourning–and in absurd, tenacious hope.

Robin Morgan is an award-winning writer, feminist leader, political theorist, journalist, and international activist.

This world of ours is 4600 million years old

It could end in an afternoon.

Words by Arundhati Roy. Graphic by Bindia Thapar

Inevitable Ring to the Unimaginable

John Pilger

If the attacks on America have their source in the Islamic world, who can really be surprised?

Two days earlier, eight people were killed in southern Iraq when British and American planes bombed civilian areas. To my knowledge, not a word appeared in the mainstream media in Britain.

An estimated 200,000 Iraqis, according to the Health Education Trust in London, died during and in the immediate aftermath of the slaughter known as the Gulf War.

This was never news that touched public consciousness in the west.

At least a million civilians, half of them children, have since died in Iraq as a result of a medieval embargo imposed by the United States and Britain.

In Pakistan and Afghanistan, the Mujahedeen, which gave birth to the fanatical Taliban, was largely the creation of the CIA.

The terrorist training camps where Osama bin Laden, now "America's most wanted man", allegedly planned his attacks, were built with American money and backing.

In Palestine, the enduring illegal occupation by Israel would have collapsed long ago were it not for US backing.

Far from being the terrorists of the world, the Islamic peoples have been its victims - principally the victims of US fundamentalism, whose power, in all its forms, military, strategic and economic, is the greatest source of terrorism on earth.

This fact is censored from the Western media, whose "coverage" at best minimises the culpability of imperial powers. Richard Falk, professor of international relations at Princeton, put it this way: "Western foreign policy is presented almost exclusively through a self-righteous, one-way legal/moral screen (with) positive images of Western values and innocence portrayed as threatened, validating a campaign of unrestricted political violence."

That Tony Blair, whose government sells lethal weapons to Israel and has sprayed Iraq and Yugoslavia with cluster bombs and depleted uranium and was the greatest arms supplier to the genocidists in Indonesia, can be taken seriously when he now speaks about the "shame" of the "new evil of mass terrorism" says much about the censorship of our collective sense of how the world is managed.

One of Blair's favourite words - "fatuous" - comes to mind. Alas, it is no comfort to the families of thousands of ordinary Americans who have died so terribly that the perpetrators of their suffering may be the product of Western policies. Did the American establishment believe that it could bankroll and manipulate events in the Middle East without cost to itself, or rather its own innocent people?

The attacks on Tuesday come at the end of a long history of betrayal of the Islamic and Arab peoples: the collapse of the Ottoman Empire, the foundation of the state of Israel, four Arab-Israeli wars and 34 years of Israel's brutal occupation of an Arab nation: all, it seems, obliterated within hours by Tuesday's acts of awesome cruelty by those who say they represent the victims of the West's intervention in their homelands.

"America, which has never known modern war, now has her own terrible league table: perhaps as many as 20,000 victims."

As Robert Fisk points out, in the Middle East, people will grieve the loss of innocent life, but they will ask if the newspapers and television networks of the west ever devoted a fraction of the present coverage to the half-a-million dead children of Iraq, and the 17,500 civilians killed in Israel's 1982 invasion of Lebanon. The answer is no. There are deeper roots to the atrocities in the US, which made them almost inevitable.

It is not only the rage and grievance in the Middle East and south Asia. Since the end of the cold war, the US and its sidekicks, principally Britain, have exercised, flaunted, and abused their wealth and power while the divisions imposed on human beings by them and their agents have grown as never before.

An elite group of less than a billion people now take more than 80 per cent of the world's wealth.

In defence of this power and privilege, known by the euphemisms "free market" and "free trade", the injustices are legion: from the illegal blockade of Cuba, to the murderous arms trade, dominated by the US, to its trashing of basic environmental decencies, to the assault on fragile economies by institutions such as the World Trade Organisation that are little more than agents of the US Treasury and the European central banks, and the demands of the World Bank and the International Monetary Fund in forcing the poorest nations to repay unrepayable debts; to a new US "Vietnam" in Colombia and the sabotage of peace talks between North and South Korea (in order to shore up North Korea's "rogue nation" status).

Western terror is part of the recent history of imperialism, a word that journalists dare not speak or write.

The expulsion of the population of Diego Garcia in the 1960s by the Wilson government received almost no press coverage.

Their homeland is now an American nuclear arms dump and base from which US bombers patrol the Middle East.

In Indonesia, in 1965/6, a million people were killed with the complicity of the US and British governments: the Americans supplying General Suharto with assassination lists, then ticking off names as people were killed.

"Getting British companies and the World Bank back in there was part of the deal", says Roland Challis, who was the BBC's south east Asia correspondent.

British behaviour in Malaya was no different from the American record in Vietnam, for which it proved inspirational: the withholding of food, villages turned into concentration camps and more than half a million people forcibly dispossessed.

In Vietnam, the dispossession, maiming and poisoning of an entire nation was apocalyptic, yet diminished in our memory by Hollywood movies and by what Edward Said rightly calls cultural imperialism.

In Operation Phoenix, in Vietnam, the CIA arranged the homicide of around 50,000 people. As official documents now reveal, this was the model for the terror in Chile that climaxed with the murder of the democratically elected leader Salvador Allende, and within 10 years, the crushing of Nicaragua.

All of it was lawless. The list is too long for this piece.

Now imperialism is being rehabilitated. American forces currently operate with impunity from bases in 50 countries.

"Full spectrum dominance" is Washington's clearly stated aim.

Read the documents of the US Space Command, which leaves us in no doubt.

In this country, the eager Blair government has embarked on four violent adventures, in pursuit of "British interests" (dressed up as "peacekeeping"), and which have little or no basis in international law: a record matched by no other British government for half a century.

What has this to do with this week's atrocities in America? If you travel among the impoverished majority of humanity, you understand that it has everything to do with it.

People are neither still, nor stupid. They see their independence compromised, their resources and land and the lives of their children taken away, and their accusing fingers increasingly point north: to the great enclaves of plunder and privilege. Inevitably, terror breeds terror and more fanaticism.

But how patient the oppressed have been.

It is only a few years ago that the Islamic fundamentalist groups, willing to blow themselves up in Israel and New York, were formed, and only after Israel and the US had rejected outright the hope of a Palestinian state, and justice for a people scarred by imperialism.

Their distant voices of rage are now heard; the daily horrors in faraway brutalised places have at last come home.

September 13, 2001

John Pilger is an award-winning journalist.

Illustration by Bindia Thapar

Black Tuesday:
The View from Islamabad

Pervez Hoodbhoy

Samuel Huntington's evil desire for a clash between civilisations may well come true after Tuesday's terror attacks. The crack that divided Muslims everywhere from the rest of the world is no longer a crack. It is a gulf that if not bridged, will surely destroy both.

For much of the world, it was the indescribable savagery of seeing jet-loads of innocent human beings piloted into buildings filled with other innocent human beings. It was the sheer horror of watching people jump from the 80th floor of the collapsing World Trade Centre rather than be consumed by the inferno inside.

Yes, it is true that many Muslims also saw it exactly this way, and felt the searing agony no less sharply. The heads of states of Muslim countries, Saddam Hussein excepted, condemned the attacks. Leaders of Muslim communities in the US, Canada, Britain, Europe, and Australia have made impassioned denunciations and pleaded for the need to distinguish between ordinary Muslims and extremists.

But the pretence that reality goes no further must be abandoned because this merely obfuscates facts and slows down the search for solutions. One would like to dismiss televised images showing Palestinian expressions of joy as unrepresentative, reflective only of the crass political immaturity of a handful. But this may be wishful thinking. Similarly, Pakistan Television, operating under strict control of the government, is attempting to portray a nation united in condemnation of the attack. Here too, the truth lies elsewhere, as I learn from students at my university here in Islamabad, from conversations with people in the streets, and from the Urdu press.

A friend tells me that crowds gathered around public TV sets at Islamabad airport had cheered as the WTC came crashing down. It makes one feel sick from inside.

A bizarre new world awaits us, where old rules of social and political behaviour have broken down and new ones are yet to be defined. Catapulted into a situation of darkness and horror by the extraordinary force of events, as rational human beings we must urgently formulate a response that is moral, and not based upon considerations of power and practicality. This requires beginning with a clearly defined moral supposition - the fundamental equality of all human beings. It also requires that we must proceed according to a definite sequence of steps, the order of which is not interchangeable.

Before all else, Black Tuesday's mass murder must be condemned in the harshest possible terms without qualification or condition, without seeking causes or reasons that may even remotely be used to justify it, and without regard for the national identity of the victims or the perpetrators. The demented, suicidal, fury of the attackers led to heinous acts of indiscriminate and wholesale murder that have changed the world for the worse. A moral position must begin with unequivocal condemnation, the absence of which could eliminate even the language by which people can communicate.

Analysis comes second, but it is just as essential. No "terrorist" gene is known to exist or is likely to be found. Therefore, surely the attackers, and their supporters, who were all presumably born normal, were afflicted by something that caused their metamorphosis from normal human beings capable of gentleness and affection into desperate, maddened, fiends with nothing but murder in their hearts and minds. What was that?

Tragically, CNN and the US media have so far made little attempt to understand this affliction. The cost for this omission, if it is to stay this way, cannot be anything but terrible. What we have seen is probably the first of similar tragedies that may come to define the 21st century as the century of terror. There is much claptrap about "fighting terrorism" and billions are likely to be poured into surveillance, fortifications, and emergency plans, not to mention the ridiculous idea of missile defence systems. But, as a handful of suicide bombers armed with no more than knives and box-cutters have shown with such devastating effectiveness, all this means precisely nothing. Modern nations are far too vulnerable to be protected - a suitcase nuclear device could flatten not just a building or two, but all of Manhattan. Therefore, the simple logic of survival says that the chances of survival are best if one goes to the roots of terror.

Only a fool can believe that the services of a suicidal terrorist can be purchased, or that they can be bred at will anywhere. Instead, their breeding grounds are in refugee camps and in other rubbish dumps of humanity, abandoned by civilisation and left to rot. A global superpower, indifferent to their plight, and manifestly on the side of their tormentors, has bred boundless hatred for its policies. In supreme arrogance, indifferent to world opinion, the US openly sanctions daily dispossession and torture of the Palestinians by Israeli occupation forces. The deafening silence over the massacres in Qana, Sabra, and Shatila refugee camps, and the video-gamed slaughter by the Pentagon of 70,000 people in Iraq, has brought out the worst that humans are capable of. In the words of Robert Fisk, "those who claim to represent a crushed, humiliated population struck back with the wickedness and awesome cruelty of a doomed people".

It is stupid and cruel to derive satisfaction from such revenge, or from the indisputable fact that Osama and his kind are the blowback of the CIAs misadventures in Afghanistan. Instead, the real question is: where do we, the inhabitants of this planet, go from here? What is the lesson to be learnt from the still smouldering ruins of the World Trade Centre? If the lesson is that America needs to assert its military might, then the future will be as grim as can be. Indeed, Secretary Colin Powell, has promised "more than a single reprisal raid". But against whom? And to what end? No one doubts that it is ridiculously easy for the US to unleash carnage. But the bodies of a few thousand dead Afghans will not bring peace, or reduce by one bit the chances of a still worse terrorist attack.

This not an argument for inaction: Osama and his gang, as well as other such gangs, if they can be found, must be brought to justice. But indiscriminate slaughter can do nothing except add fuel to existing hatreds. Today, the US is the victim but the carpet-bombing of Afghanistan will cause it to squander the huge swell of sympathy in its favour the world over. Instead, it will create nothing but revulsion and promote never-ending tit-for-tat killings.

Ultimately, the security of the United States lies in its re-engaging with the people of the world, especially with those that it has grievously harmed. As a great country, possessing an admirable constitution that protects the life and liberty of its citizens, it must extend its definition of humanity to cover all peoples of the world. It must respect international treaties such as those on greenhouse gases and biological weapons, stop trying to force a new Cold War by pushing through NMD, pay its UN dues, and cease the aggrandisement of wealth in the name of globalisation.

But it is not only the US that needs to learn new modes of behaviour. There are important lessons for Muslims too, particularly those living in the US, Canada, and Europe. Last year I heard the arch-conservative head of Pakistan's Jamat-i-Islami, Qazi Husain Ahmad, begin his lecture before an American audience in Washington with high praise for a "pluralist society where I can wear the clothes I like, pray at a mosque, and preach my religion". Certainly, such freedoms do not exist for religious minorities in Pakistan, or in most Muslim countries. One hopes that the misplaced anger against innocent Muslims dissipates soon and such freedoms are not curtailed significantly. Nevertheless, there is a serious question as to whether this pluralism can persist forever, and if it does not, whose responsibility it will be.

The problem is that immigrant Muslim communities have, by and large, chosen isolation over integration. In the long run this is a fundamentally unhealthy situation because it creates suspicion and friction, and makes living together ever so much harder. It also raises serious ethical questions about drawing upon the resources of what is perceived to be another society, for which one has hostile feelings. This is not an argument for doing away with one's Muslim identity. But, without closer interaction with the mainstream, pluralism will be threatened. Above all, survival of the community depends upon strongly emphasising the difference between extremists and ordinary Muslims, and on purging from within jihadist elements committed to violence. Any member of the Muslim community who thinks that ordinary people in the US are fair game because of bad US government policies has no business being there.

To echo George W. Bush, "let there be no mistake". But here the mistake will be to let the heart rule the head in the aftermath of utter horror, to bomb a helpless Afghan people into an even earlier period of the Stone Age, or to take similar actions that originate from the spine. Instead, in deference to a billion years of patient evolution, we need to hand over charge to the cerebellum. Else, survival of this particular species is far from guaranteed.

Pervez Hoodbhoy is professor of physics at Quaid-e-Azam University, Islamabad.

You are asking for a Nuclear bomb to bring peace in the region.
Why don't you ask for peace itself.

Illustration by C F John

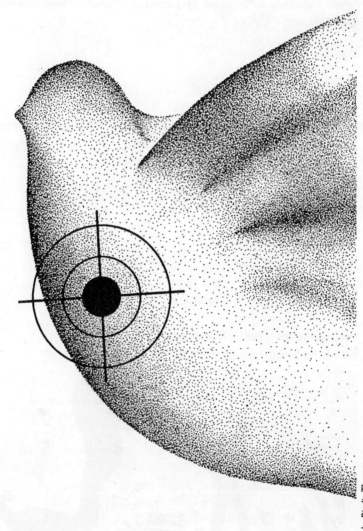

Illustration by Bindia Thapar

Endless War?

Walden Bello

The assault on the World Trade Centre was horrific, despicable, and unpardonable, but it is important not to lose perspective, especially a historical one. For a response that is dictated primarily by fury such as that now displayed by some American politicians, while understandable, is likely to simply serve as one more proof for Santayana's dictum that those who do not remember history are bound to repeat it.

The Moral Equation

The scale and consequences of the World Trade Centre attack are massive indeed, but this was not the worst act of mass terrorism in US history, as some US media are wont to claim. The over 5000 lives lost in New York are irreplaceable, but one must not forget that the atomic raids on Hiroshima and Nagasaki killed 210,000 people, most of them civilians, most perishing instantaneously. But one may object that you can't really compare the World Trade Centre attack to the nuclear bombings since, after all, Hiroshima and Nagasaki were targets in a war. But why not, since the purpose of the nuclear bombings was not mainly to destroy military or infrastructural targets, but to terrorise and destroy the civilian population? Indeed, the whole allied air campaign against Germany and Japan in 1944-45, which produced the firestorms in Dresden, Hamburg, and Tokyo, that killed tens of thousands had as its central aim to kill and maim as many civilians as possible. Similarly, during the Korean War, terror bombing of civilians was the policy of the US Air Force's Far Eastern Command, which was instructed to pulverise anything that moved in enemy territory. So successful was the policy that in the summer of 1951, the commander was able to report that "there is no structure left to be targeted."

During the Cold War, mass elimination of the enemy's civilian population, alongside the destruction of his armed forces or industry, was institutionalised in the strategy of massive nuclear retaliation that lay at the centre of the doctrine of Deterrence. In Vietnam, where the US was frustrated by the fact that combatants and civilians were indistinguishable, indiscriminate killing of civilians was a central part of a "counterinsurgency war" in which 20,000 civilians were systematically assassinated under the CIA's Operation Phoenix Program in the Mekong Delta.

But must not such actions against civilians be judged in the context of a broader strategic objective of sapping the enemy's will to fight and thus bring the war to a conclusion? But then how different is this justification from the terrorists' aim to change the foreign policy of the US government by eroding the support of the country's civilian population?

The point is not to engage in a "maleficent calculus," as Jeremy Bentham would have called this exercise, but to point out that the US government hardly possesses the high ground in the current moral equation. Indeed, one can say that terrorists like Osama bin Laden, an ex-CIA protégé, have learned their lessons on the strategic targeting of the civilian population from Washington's traditional strategy of total warfare, where damage to the civilian population is not simply seen as collateral but as essential to achieving the ends of war.

The Clausewitzian Calculus

In the aftermath of the World Trade Centre assault, the perpetrators of the dastardly deed have been called "irrational" or "madmen" or people that embody evil. This is understandable as an emotional reaction but dangerous as a basis for policy. The truth is the perpetrators of the deed were very rational. If they were indeed people connected with Osama bin Laden, their goal was most likely to raise the costs to the United States of maintaining its current policies in the Middle East, which they consider unjust and inequitable, and this was their way of doing it. They very rationally picked the targets and weapons to be used, paying attention not only to maximum destruction but also to maximum symbolism. The choice of the World Trade Centre towers and the Pentagon as the targets, and American Airlines and United Airlines planes as the delivery vehicles doubling as warheads, was the product of cold-blooded thinking and planning. The loss of their own lives was factored into the calculation. What we saw was a rational calculus of means to achieve a desired end. In the view of these people, terrorism, like war, is the extension of politics by other means. These are Clausewitzian minds, and the worst mistake one can make is to regard them as lunatics.

Pearl Harbour Or Tet?

One metaphor that the Washington establishment has used to capture the essence of recent events is that of a second Pearl Harbour, with the implication that, like the first, the September 11 tragedy will galvanise the American people to an unprecedented level of unity to win the war against still unidentified enemies. The other side, one suspects, operates with a different metaphor, and this is that of the Tet Offensive of 1968. The objective of the Vietnamese was to launch massive simultaneous uprisings that, even if defeated separately, would nevertheless add up to a strategic victory by convincing the other side, especially its civilian base, that the war was unwinnable. The aim was to rob the US of the will to win the war, and here the Vietnamese succeeded.

The perpetrators of World Trade Centre assault are operating with a similar calculus, and, despite the current jingoistic talk in Washington, it is not certain that they are wrong. Will the American people really bear any burden and pay any price in a struggle that will persist way into the future, with no assurance of victory, indeed, with no clear sense of who the enemies are and of what "victory" will consist of?

The media is full of news about the creation of an alliance against terrorism, conveying the impression that co-ordination among key states combined with the outrage of citizens everywhere will give a Washington-led coalition an unbeatable edge. Perhaps in the short run, although even this is not certain. For the problem is that, as in guerrilla wars, this is not a war that will be won strictly or mainly by military means.

The Underlying Issues

If it was bin Laden's network that was responsible for the World

Trade Centre attack, then the underlying issues are the twin pillars of US policy in the Middle East. One is subordination of the interests of the peoples of the region to the US' untrammelled access to Middle East oil in order to maintain its petroleum-based civilisation. To this end, the US overthrew the nationalist government of Mossadegh in Iran in 1953, cultivated the repressive Shah of Iran as the gendarme of the Persian Gulf, supported anti-democratic feudal regimes in the Arabian peninsula, and introduced a massive permanent military presence in Saudi Arabia, which contains some of Islam's most sacred shrines and cities.

The war against Saddam Hussein was justified as a war to beat back aggression, but everybody knew that Washington's key motivation was to ensure that the region's most massive oil reserves would remain under the control of pro-Western elites.

The other pillar is unstinting support for Israel. That Arab feelings about Israel are so elemental is not difficult to comprehend. It is hard to argue against the fact that the state of Israel was born on the basis of the massive dispossession of the Palestinian people from their country and their lands. It is impossible to deny that Israel is a European settler-state, one whose establishment was essentially a displacement from European territory of the ethno-cultural contradictions of European society. The Holocaust was an unspeakable crime against humanity, but it was utterly wrong to impose its political consequences—chief of which was the creation of Israel—on a people who had nothing to do with it.

It is hard to contradict Arab claims that it was essentially support from the United States that created the state of Israel; that it has been massive US military aid and backing that has maintained it in the last half century; and that it is deep confidence in perpetual US military and political support that enables Israel to oppose in practice the emergence of a viable Palestinian state.

Unless the US abandons these two pillars of its policies, there will always be thousands of recruits for acts of terrorism such as that which occurred last week. And while we may condemn terrorist acts—as we must, strongly—it is another thing to expect desperate people not to adopt them, especially when they can point to the fact that it was such methods that targeted civilians as well as military personnel, combined with the Intifada, that forced Israel to agree to the 1993 Oslo Accord that led to the creation of the Palestinian entity.

Yet another reason why the strategic equation does not favour the US is that there are a great many people in the world that are ambivalent about terrorism. In contrast to Europe, there has been a relatively muted response to the World Trade Centre event in the South. A survey would probably reveal that while many people in the Third World are appalled by hijackers' methods, they are not unsympathetic to their objectives. As one Chinese-Filipino entrepreneur said, "It's horrible, but on the other hand, the US had it coming." If this reaction is common among middle class people, it would not be surprising if such ambivalence towards terrorism is widespread among the 80 per cent of the world's population that are marginalised by current global political and economic arrangements.

There is simply too much distrust, dislike, or just plain hatred of a country that has become so callous in its pursuit of economic power and arrogant in its political and military relations with the rest of the world and so brazen in declaring its cultural superiority over the rest of us. As in the equation of guerrilla war, civilian ambivalence in the theatre of battle translates strategically to a minus when it comes to the staying power of the authorities and a plus when it comes to that of the terrorists.

In sum, if there is one thing we can be certain of, it is that massive retaliation on the part of the US will not put an end to terrorism. It will simply amplify the upward spiral of violence, as the other side will resort to even more spectacular deeds, fed by unending waves of recruits. The September 11 tragedy is the clearest evidence of the bankruptcy of the 30-year-old policy of mailed fist, massive retaliation response to terrorism. This policy has simply resulted in the extreme professionalisation of terrorism.

The only response that will really contribute to global security and peace is for Washington to address not the symptoms but the roots of terrorism. It is for the United States to re-examine and substantially change its policies in the Middle East and the Third World, supporting for a change arrangements that will not stand in the way of the achievement of equity, justice, and genuine national sovereignty for currently marginalised peoples. Any other way leads to endless war.

Walden Bello is Director, Focus for the Global South, Bangkok

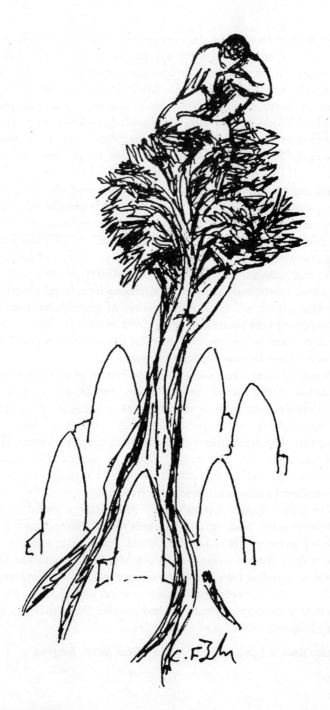

Illustration by C F John

The US, the West and the Rest of the World

Johan Galtung and Dietrich Fischer

The world will never be the same again after the terrible attack on the economic US, the military US, the foreign policy US, and on human beings like all of us. We embrace the victims of the violence, of all violence, in deep grief, and express our hope that perpetrators will be brought to justice.

A violence at this level can only be explained by a very high level of dehumanisation of the victims in the minds of the aggressors, often due to a very deep level of unresolved, basic conflict. The word "terrorism" may describe the tactics, but like "state terrorism" only portrays the perpetrator as evil, satanic, and does not go to the roots of the conflict.

The text of targets reads like a retaliation for US use of economic power against poor countries and poor people, US use of military power against defenceless people and US political power against the powerless. This calls to mind the many countries around the world where the US has bombed or otherwise exercised its awesome power, directly or indirectly; adding the 100,000 dying daily at the bottom of an economic system identified by many with US economic, military and political power. Given the millions, not thousands, of victims it has to be expected that this generates a desire for retaliation somewhere, some time.

The basic dividing line in this conflict is class, of countries and of people. It is not civilisation, although US sense of mission, manifest destiny, and Islamic sense of righteousness are parts of it. Right now the confrontation seems to be between the US/West and Arabs/Muslims. But this may also be a fallacy of misplaced concreteness: the latter may possess more intention and more capability than other victims of the enormous US/West violence since the Second world war. We should neither underestimate the extent of solidarity in the "rest of the world", nor the solidarity of the world upper class: the West; and build solidarity with victims everywhere.

In placing the horrendous attack on the US in the context of a cycle of retaliation, there is no element of justification, no excuse, no guilt-attribution. There is only deep regret that this chain of violence and retaliation is a human fact. But it may also serve to make us break that vicious spiral.

There has been an outpouring of sympathy and offers of help, even from governments with whom the US has had differences, like Russia, China, Iran, Cuba and Libya. There is an overwhelming desire to end such atrocities, in the way piracy on the high seas largely ended when all governments began to co-operate in opposing it and pirates lost their safe havens.

More stringent security measures like guards on aeroplanes, tighter surveillance of communications and sharing of intelligence can make some difference, but they do not go to the root. Bombing Afghanistan may kill some terrorists, but will also kill innocent civilians, and is likely to recruit many more who are eager to become "martyrs."

We need to eliminate weapons of mass destruction under stringent international verification, or they will be used sooner or later by terrorists, because they are not deterred by the threat of retaliation.

With talk of Crusades from the USA, and of the fourth stage of jihad, Holy War, from Islamic quarters, the world may beheading for the largest violent encounter ever. The first jihad, against the Crusades 1095-1291 lasted 196 years; the Muslims won. The second, against Israel, is undecided. The third, against communism in Afghanistan, supported by the US, ended with Soviet withdrawal and collapse. Some Muslims are willing to die for their faith, expecting to go to paradise. Yet most Muslim clerics have stressed that the Koran prohibits the taking of innocent lives. Equating all Muslims with terrorists would be like equating all Christians with the Ku Klux Klan.

To prevent a slide into a large war with enormous, widespread suffering, the US, everybody, should not rush to action. There is a need for deep self-reflection, seeking to identify the conflicts, the issues, solve them, reconcile. Dialogue and global education to understand how others think, and to respect other cultures, not

debate to defeat others with stronger arguments, can lead the way toward healing and closure.

Governments in the West, and also in the South, cannot be relied upon to do this; they are too tied to the US and also too afraid of incurring US wrath. Only people can, only the global civil society. What is needed as soon as humanly possible is a massive peace movement, this time North-South. It worked last time, East-West. The future of the world is more than ever in the hands of the only source of legitimacy: people everywhere.

A Chinese proverb says, "If a spear is sticking in someone's body, it is not enough to break off the visible part. Unless the tip is removed from inside the body, a festering wound will persist." As painful as it is for many at this time of tragedy, if we want to succeed in eliminating terrorism, we must understand its sources and remove the causes of extreme hatred that drive some people to commit mass murder and suicide.

Johan Galtung, a Professor of Peace Studies, is Director of TRANSCEND, a peace and development network. Dietrich Fischer, a Professor at Pace University, is co-director of TRANSCEND.

Illustration by Bindia Thapar

Experts we are
In mending and darning
Give us the globe
Heed the Warning!

Words by Kamla Bhasin. Illustration by Yoko Kihira

Between Reality and Self-righteousness

Susan Sontag

The disconnect between last Tuesday's monstrous dose of reality and the self-righteous drivel and outright deceptions being peddled by public figures and TV commentators is startling, depressing. The voices licensed to follow the event seem to have joined together in a campaign to infantilise the public. Where is the acknowledgement that this was not a "cowardly" attack on "civilisation" or "liberty" or "humanity" or "the free world" but an attack on the world's self-proclaimed superpower, undertaken as a consequence of specific American alliances and actions?

How many citizens are aware of the ongoing American bombing of Iraq? And if the word "cowardly" is to be used, it might be more aptly applied to those who kill from beyond the range of retaliation, high in the sky, than to those willing to die themselves in order to kill others. In the matter of courage (a morally neutral virtue): whatever may be said of the perpetrators of Tuesday's slaughter, they were not cowards.

Our leaders are bent on convincing us that everything is OK America is not afraid. Our spirit is unbroken, although this was a day that will live in infamy and America is now at war. But everything is not OK And this was not Pearl Harbour. We have a robotic President who assures us that America still stands tall. A wide spectrum of public figures, in and out of office, who are strongly opposed to the policies being pursued abroad by this Administration apparently feel free to say nothing more than that they stand united behind President Bush. A lot of thinking needs to be done, and perhaps is being done in Washington and elsewhere, about the ineptitude of American intelligence and counter-intelligence, about options available to American foreign policy, particularly in the Middle East, and about what constitutes a smart program of military defence. But the public is not being asked to bear much of the burden of reality. The unanimously applauded, self-congratulatory bromides of a Soviet Party Congress seemed contemptible. The unanimity of the sanctimonious, reality-concealing rhetoric spouted by American officials and media commentators in recent days seems, well, unworthy of a mature democracy.

Those in public office have let us know that they consider their task to be a manipulative one: confidence-building and grief management. Politics, the politics of a democracy - which entails disagreement, which promotes candour - has been replaced by psychotherapy. Let's by all means grieve together. But let's not be stupid together. A few shreds of historical awareness might help us understand what has just happened, and what may continue to happen. "Our country is strong," we are told again and again. I for one don't find this entirely consoling. Who doubts that America is strong? But that's not all America has to be.

Susan Sontag is one of America's finest political essayists.

Illustration by Bindia Thapar

Conversations with Noam Chomsky

Why do you think these attacks happened?

To answer the question we must first identify the perpetrators of the crimes. It is generally assumed, plausibly, that their origin is the Middle East region, and that the attacks probably trace back to the Osama bin Laden network, a widespread and complex organisation, doubtless inspired by bin Laden but not necessarily acting under his control. Let us assume that this is true. Then to answer your question a sensible person would try to ascertain bin Laden's views, and the sentiments of the large reservoir of supporters he has throughout the region. About all of this, we have a great deal of information. Bin Laden has been interviewed extensively over the years by highly reliable Middle East specialists, notably the most eminent correspondent in the region, Robert Fisk (*The Independent*, London), who has intimate knowledge of the entire region and direct experience over decades. A Saudi Arabian millionaire, bin Laden became a militant Islamic leader in the war to drive the Russians out of Afghanistan. He was one of the many religious fundamentalist extremists recruited, armed, and financed by the CIA and their allies in Pakistani intelligence to cause maximal harm to the Russians – quite possibly delaying their withdrawal, many analysts suspect – though whether he personally happened to have direct contact with the CIA is unclear, and not particularly important. Not surprisingly, the CIA preferred the most fanatic and cruel fighters they could mobilise. The end result was to "destroy a moderate regime and create a fanatical one, from groups recklessly financed by the Americans" (*London Times* correspondent Simon Jenkins, also a specialist on the region). These "Afghanis" as they are called (many, like bin Laden, not from Afghanistan) carried out terror operations across the border in Russia, but they terminated these after Russia withdrew. Their war was not against Russia, which they despise, but against the Russian occupation and Russia's crimes against Muslims.

The "Afghanis" did not terminate their activities, however. They joined Bosnian Muslim forces in the Balkan Wars; the US did not object, just as it tolerated Iranian support for them, for complex reasons that we need not pursue here, apart from noting that concern for the grim fate of the Bosnians was not prominent among them. The "Afghanis" are also fighting the Russians in Chechnya, and, quite possibly, are involved in carrying out terrorist attacks in Moscow and elsewhere in Russian territory. Bin Laden and his "Afghanis" turned against the US in 1990 when they established permanent bases in Saudi Arabia – from his point of view, a counterpart to the Russian occupation of Afghanistan, but far more significant because of Saudi Arabia's special status as the guardian of the holiest shrines.

Bin Laden is also bitterly opposed to the corrupt and repressive regimes of the region, which he regards as "un-Islamic," including the Saudi Arabian regime, the most extreme Islamic fundamentalist regime in the world, apart from the Taliban, and a close US ally since its origins. Bin Laden despises the US for its support of these regimes. Like others in the region, he is also outraged by long-standing US support for Israel's brutal military occupation, now in its 35th year: Washington's decisive diplomatic, military, and economic intervention in support of the killings, the harsh and destructive siege over many years, the daily humiliation to which Palestinians are subjected, the expanding settlements designed to break the occupied territories into Bantustan-like cantons and take control of the resources, the gross violation of the Geneva Conventions, and other actions that are recognised as crimes throughout most of the world, apart from the US, which has prime responsibility for them. And like others, he contrasts Washington's dedicated support for these crimes with the decade-long US-British assault against the civilian population of Iraq, which has devastated the society and caused hundreds of thousands of deaths while strengthening Saddam Hussein – who was a favoured friend and ally of the US and Britain right through his worst atrocities, including the gassing of the Kurds, as people of the region also remember well, even if Westerners prefer to forget the facts. These sentiments are very widely shared. *The Wall Street Journal* (Sept. 14) published a survey of opinions of wealthy and privileged Muslims in the Gulf region (bankers, professionals, businessmen with close links to the US). They expressed much the same views: resentment of the US policies of supporting Israeli crimes and blocking the international consensus on a diplomatic settlement for many years while devastating Iraqi civilian society, supporting harsh and repressive anti-democratic regimes throughout the region, and imposing barriers against economic development by "propping up oppressive regimes." Among the great majority of people suffering deep poverty and oppression, similar sentiments are far more bitter, and are the source of the fury and despair that has led to suicide bombings, as commonly understood by those who are interested in the facts.

The US, and much of the West, prefers a more comforting story. To quote the lead analysis in the *New York Times* (Sept. 16), the perpetrators acted out of "hatred for the values cherished in the West as freedom, tolerance, prosperity, religious pluralism and universal suffrage." US actions are irrelevant, and therefore need not even be mentioned (Serge Schmemann). This is a convenient picture, and the general stance is not unfamiliar in intellectual history; in fact, it is close to the norm. It happens to be completely at variance with everything we know, but has all the merits of self-adulation and uncritical support for power.

It is also widely recognised that bin Laden and others like him are praying for "a great assault on Muslim states," which will cause "fanatics to flock to his cause" (Jenkins, and many others.). That too is familiar. The escalating cycle of violence is typically welcomed by the harshest and most brutal elements on both sides, a fact evident enough from the recent history of the Balkans, to cite only one of many cases.

What consequences will they have on US inner policy and to the American self-reception?

US policy has already been officially announced. The world is being offered a "stark choice": join us, or "face the certain prospect of death and destruction." Congress has authorised the use of force against any individuals or countries the President determines to be involved in the attacks, a doctrine that every supporter regards as ultra-criminal. That is easily demonstrated. Simply ask how the same people would have reacted if Nicaragua had adopted this doctrine after the US had rejected the orders of the World Court to terminate its "unlawful use of force" against Nicaragua and had vetoed a Security Council resolution calling on all states to observe international law. And that terrorist attack was far more severe and destructive even than this atrocity.

As for how these matters are perceived here, that is far more complex. One should bear in mind that the media and the intellectual elites generally have their particular agendas. Furthermore, the answer to this question is, in significant measure, a matter of decision: as in many other cases, with sufficient dedication and energy, efforts to stimulate fanaticism, blind hatred, and submission to authority can be reversed. We all know that very well.

Do you expect US to profoundly change their policy to the rest of the world?

The initial response was to call for intensifying the policies that led to the fury and resentment that provides the background of support for the terrorist attack, and to pursue more intensively the agenda of the most hard line elements of the leadership: increased militarisation, domestic regimentation, attack on social programs. That is all to be expected. Again, terror attacks, and the escalating cycle of violence they often engender, tend to reinforce the authority and prestige of the most harsh and repressive elements of a society. But there is nothing inevitable about submission to this course.

After the first shock, came fear of what the US answer is going to be. Are you afraid, too?

Every sane person should be afraid of the likely reaction – the one that has already been announced, the one that probably answers Bin Laden's prayers. It is highly likely to escalate the cycle of violence, in the familiar way, but in this case on a far greater scale.

The US has already demanded that Pakistan terminate the food and other supplies that are keeping at least some of the starving and suffering people of Afghanistan alive. If that demand is implemented, unknown numbers of people who have not the remotest connection to terrorism will die, possibly millions. Let me repeat: the US has demanded that Pakistan kill possibly millions of people who are themselves victims of the Taliban. This has nothing to do even with revenge. It is at a far lower moral level even than that. The significance is heightened by the fact that this is mentioned in passing, with no comment, and probably will hardly be noticed. We can learn a great deal about the moral level of the reigning intellectual culture of the West by observing the reaction to this demand. I think we can be reasonably confident that if the American population had the slightest idea of what is being done in their name, they would be utterly appalled. It would be instructive to seek historical precedents.

If Pakistan does not agree to this and other US demands, it may come under direct attack as well – with unknown consequences. If Pakistan does submit to US demands, it is not impossible that the government will be overthrown by forces much like the Taliban – who in this case will have nuclear weapons. That could have an effect throughout the region, including the oil producing states. At this point we are considering the possibility of a war that may destroy much of human society.

Even without pursuing such possibilities, the likelihood is that an attack on Afghans will have pretty much the effect that most analysts expect: it will enlist great numbers of others to support of bin Laden, as he hopes. Even if he is killed, it will make little difference. His voice will be heard on cassettes that are distributed throughout the Islamic world, and he is likely to be revered as a martyr, inspiring others. It is worth bearing in mind that one suicide bombing – a truck driven into a US military base – drove the world's major military force out of Lebanon 20 years ago. The opportunities for such attacks are endless. And suicide attacks are very hard to prevent.

"The world will never be the same after 11.09.01". Do you think so?

The horrendous terrorist attacks on Tuesday are something quite new in world affairs, not in their scale and character, but in the target. For the US, this is the first time since the War of 1812 that its national territory has been under attack, even threat. Its colonies have been attacked, but not the national territory itself. During these years the US virtually exterminated the indigenous population, conquered half of Mexico, intervened violently in the surrounding region, conquered Hawaii and the Philippines (killing hundreds of thousands of Filipinos), and in the past half century particularly, extended its resort to force throughout much of the world. The number of victims is colossal. For the first time, the guns have been directed the other way. The same is true, even more dramatically, of Europe. Europe has suffered murderous destruction, but from internal wars, meanwhile conquering much of the world with extreme brutality. It has not been under attack by its victims outside, with rare exceptions (the IRA in England, for example). It is therefore natural that NATO should rally to the support of the US; hundreds of years of imperial violence have an enormous impact on the intellectual and moral culture.

It is correct to say that this is a novel event in world history, not because of the scale of the atrocity – regrettably – but because of the target. How the West chooses to react is a matter of supreme importance. If the rich and powerful choose to keep to their traditions of hundreds of years and resort to extreme violence, they will contribute to the escalation of a cycle of violence, in a familiar dynamic, with long-term consequences that could be awesome. Of course, that is by no means inevitable. An aroused public within the more free and democratic societies can direct policies towards a much more humane and honourable course.

According to you, an attack against Afghanistan, is "a war against terrorism"?

An attack against Afghanistan will probably kill a great many innocent civilians, not Taliban but their victims, possibly enormous numbers in a country where millions are already on the verge of death from starvation. It will also answer bin Laden's most fervent prayers, as Washington is hearing from foreign leaders, specialists on the region, and presumably it's own intelligence agencies. Such an attack will be a massive crime in itself, and will very likely escalate the cycle of violence, including new acts of terror directed against the West, possibly with consequences even more horrifying than those of September 11. The dynamics are, after all, very familiar.

Can we talk of the clash between two civilisations?

This is fashionable talk, but it makes little sense. Suppose we briefly review some familiar history.

The most populous Islamic state is Indonesia, a favourite of the US ever since Suharto took power in 1965, as army-led massacres slaughtered hundreds of thousands of people, mostly landless peasants, with the assistance of the US and with an outburst of euphoria from the West that was unconstrained, and is so embarrassing in retrospect that it has been effectively wiped out of memory. Suharto remained "our kind of guy," as the Clinton administration called him, as he compiled one of the most horrendous records of slaughter, torture, and other abuses of the late 20th century. The most extreme Islamic fundamentalist state, apart from the Taliban, is Saudi Arabia, a US client since its founding. In the 1980s, the US along with Pakistani intelligence (helped by Saudi Arabia, Britain, and others), recruited, armed, and trained the most extreme Islamic fundamentalists they could find to cause maximal harm to the Russians in Afghanistan. As Simon Jenkins observes in the *London Times*, those efforts "destroyed a moderate regime and created a fanatical one, from groups recklessly financed by the Americans." One of the beneficiaries was Osama bin Laden. Also in the 1980s, the US and UK gave strong support to their friend and ally Saddam Hussein – more secular, to be sure, but on the Islamic side of the "clash" – right through the period of his worst atrocities, including the gassing of the Kurds, and beyond.

Also in the 1980s the US fought a major war in Central America, leaving some 200,000 tortured and mutilated corpses, millions of orphans and refugees, and four countries devastated. A prime target of the US attack was the Catholic Church, which had offended the self-described "civilised world" by adopting "the preferential option for the poor."

In the early 90s, primarily for cynical great power reasons, the US selected Bosnian Muslims as their Balkan clients, to their enormous harm.

Without continuing, exactly where do we find the divide between "civilisations." Are we to conclude that there is a "clash of civilisations" with the Catholic Church on one side, and the US and the most murderous and fanatic religious fundamentalists of the Islamic world on the other side? I do not of course suggest any such absurdity. But exactly what are we to conclude, on rational grounds?

Do you think we are using the word civilisation properly? Would a really civilised world lead us to a global war like this?

It is said that Gandhi was once asked what he thought of Western civilisation, and answered that he felt it might be a good idea. No civilised society would tolerate anything I have just mentioned, which is of course only a tiny sample even of US history, and European history is even worse. And surely no "civilised world" would plunge the world into a major war instead of following the means prescribed by international law, following ample precedents.

Do you condemn terrorism? How can we decide which act is terrorism and which one is an act of resistance of a desperate nation against a tyrant or an occupying force? In which of the previous categories do you "classify" the recent strike against USA?

I understand the term "terrorism" exactly in the sense defined in official US documents: "the calculated use of violence or threat of violence to attain goals that are political, religious, or ideological in nature. This is done through intimidation, coercion, or instilling fear."

In accord with this – entirely appropriate – definition, the recent attack on the US is certainly an act of terrorism, in fact, a horrifying terrorist crime. There is scarcely any disagreement about this throughout the world, nor should there be.

But alongside the literal meaning of the term, as just quoted from us official documents, there is also a propagandistic usage, which unfortunately is the standard one: the term "terrorism" is used to refer to terrorist acts committed by enemies against us or our allies. Political scientist Michael Stohl is quite correct when he writes that "we must recognise that by convention – and it must be emphasised only by convention – great power use and the threat of the use of force is normally described as coercive diplomacy and not as a form of terrorism," though it commonly involves "the threat and often the use of violence for what would be described as terroristic purposes were it not great powers who were pursuing the very same tactic."

This propagandistic use is virtually universal. Everyone "condemns terrorism," in this sense of the term. The Nazis harshly condemned terrorism, and carried out counter-terrorism against the terrorist partisans – in Greece, for example. The US basically agreed.

It organised and conducted similar "counter-terrorism" in Greece and elsewhere in the post-war years. Furthermore, US counterinsurgency programs drew quite explicitly from the Nazi model, which was treated with respect: Wehrmacht officers were consulted and their manuals were used in designing post-war counterinsurgency programs world-wide, typically called "counter-terrorism."

Given these conventions, even the very same people and actions can quickly shift from "terrorists" to "freedom fighters" and back again. That's been happening right next door to Greece in recent years. The kla-uck were officially condemned by the US as "terrorists" in 1998, because of their attacks on Serb police and civilians in an effort to elicit a disproportionate and brutal Serbian response, as they openly declared. As late as January 1999, the British – the most hawkish element in NATO on this matter – believed that the kla-uck was responsible for more deaths than Serbia, which is hard to believe, but at least tells us something about perceptions at high levels in NATO. If one can trust the voluminous documentation provided by the state department, NATO, the OSCE, and other western sources, nothing materially changed on the ground until the withdrawal of the KVM monitors and the bombing in late march 1999. But policies did change: the US and UK decided to launch an attack on Serbia, and the "terrorists" instantly became "freedom fighters." after the war, they became "terrorists," "thugs," and "murderers" as they carried out similar actions in Macedonia, a US ally.

Everyone condemns terrorism, but we have to ask what they mean. You can find the answer to your question about my views in many books and articles that I have written about terrorism in the past several decades, though I use the term in the literal sense, and hence condemn all terrorist actions, not only those that are called "terrorist" for propagandistic reasons.

It should be unnecessary to point out that massive terrorism is a standard device of powerful states, just as Stohl observes. Some cases are not even controversial. Take the us war against Nicaragua, leaving tens of thousands dead and the country in ruins. Nicaragua appealed to the world court, which condemned the us for international terrorism ("the unlawful use of force"), ordering it to desist and pay substantial reparations. The us responded to the court ruling by sharply escalating the war, and vetoing a security council resolution calling on all states to observe international law. The escalation included official orders to attack "soft targets" – undefended civilian targets, like agricultural collectives and health clinics – and to avoid the Nicaraguan army. The terrorists were able to carry out these instructions, thanks to the completely control of Nicaraguan air space by the us and the advanced communications equipment provided to them by their supervisors.

It should also be recognised that these terrorist actions were widely approved. One prominent commentator, Michael Kinsley, at the liberal extreme of the mainstream, argued that we should not simply dismiss state department justifications for terrorist attacks on "soft targets": a "sensible policy" must "meet the test of cost-benefit analysis," an analysis of "the amount of blood and misery that will be poured in, and the likelihood that democracy will emerge at the other end" – "democracy" as the US understands the term, an interpretation illustrated quite clearly in the region. It is taken for granted that US elites have the right to conduct the analysis and pursue the project if it passes their tests. When the terrorist project succeeded, and Nicaragua succumbed, Americans were "united in joy," the New York Times proclaimed, knowing full well how the goal was achieved. As Time magazine put it joyfully, the methods were to "wreck the economy and prosecute a long and deadly proxy war until the exhausted natives overthrow the unwanted government themselves," with a cost to us that is "minimal," leaving the victim "with wrecked bridges, sabotaged power stations, and ruined farms," and thus providing the us candidate with "a winning issue": ending the "impoverishment of the people of Nicaragua." euphoria over the achievement was unconstrained among elites.

But the US terrorist war was not "terrorism," it was "counter-terrorism" by doctrinal standards. And us standards prevail in much of the world, as a result of us power and the cost of defying it.

This is by no means the most extreme example; I mention it because it is uncontroversial, given the world court decision, and because the failed efforts of Nicaragua to pursue lawful means, instead of setting off bombs in Washington, provide a model for today, not the only one.

How do you see the imminent future? What do you expect to happen now?

The US might follow the course it has proclaimed, attacking Afghanistan and probably killing a great many innocent civilians, not Taliban but their victims, possibly enormous numbers in a country where millions are already on the verge of death from starvation. By doing so, it will also answer bin Laden's most fervent prayers, as Washington is hearing from foreign leaders, specialists on the region, and presumably it's own intelligence agencies. Such an attack will be a massive crime in itself, and will very likely escalate the cycle of violence, including new acts of terror directed against the West, possibly with consequences even more horrifying than those of September 11. The dynamics are, after all, very familiar.

Or, the US might heed the warnings that it is receiving, for example, from the French foreign minister, who warned that the US would be falling into a "diabolical trap" set by bin Laden if it massacred innocents in Afghanistan.

I would not venture a prediction. But there clearly are choices within the spectrum just indicated.

Noam Chomsky is a leading political scholar at MIT.

The above text is based on several interviews given by him since September 11. We are particularly grateful to interviewers Svetlana Vukovic and Svetlana Lukic of Radio B92, Belgrade.

WAR IS NO ANSWER

Illustration by Bindia Thapar

Illustration by C F John

Dear Civilised People

Sahir Ludhyanwi

Be this blood ours or theirs
Humanity is bloodied
Be this war in East or West
A peaceful earth is bloodied
Whether the bombs fall on homes or borders
The spirit of construction is wounded
Whether it is our fields that burn or theirs
Life is wracked by starvation
It matters not that tanks advance or retreat
The womb of the earth becomes barren
Be it a celebration of victory or loss' lament
The living must mourn the corpses
That is why, O! civilised people
It is better that war remains postponed
In yours homes, and in ours
It is better that lamps continue to flicker

Illustration by C F John

Reflections on September 11, 2001

Arjun Makhijani

"Through violence you may murder a murderer, but you can't murder murder. Through violence you may murder a liar, but you can't establish truth. Through violence you may murder a hater, but you can't murder hate. Darkness cannot put out darkness. Only light can do that."

Martin Luther King, Jr.

"An eye for an eye only ends up making the whole world blind. Satyagraha is a process of educating public opinion, such that it covers all the elements of the society and makes itself irresistible. Satyagraha is a relentless search for truth and a determination to search truth. Satyagraha is an attribute of the spirit within. Satyagraha has been designed as an effective substitute for violence."

Mahatma Gandhi

The destruction of the World Trade Center towers and a part of the Pentagon on September 11, 2001, was more than an attack on the symbols of financial and military power of the United States. It was more than what the media have called an "Attack on America." It was mass murder of people from around the world. The flames of fear and sorrow and tears spread rapidly across the oceans and north and south across the Americas that day. US as well as international phone lines to New York and Washington were jammed. People from more than fifty countries were among those who perished along with thousands of Americans. No goal, however lofty, can justify the murder of innocent people.

People from around the world are grieving and share the immense sadness of the families and friends of the victims of the tragedies. The staff of the Institute for Energy and Environmental Research (IEER) grieves with them. I have written this message and these suggestions for resistance to violence and terror and militarism at the instance of and on behalf of the entire IEER staff.

The September 11 events of global terror cry out for and deserve a global response to help make the world as secure as we can from the threat of mass destruction. This was not the first or the most devastating event of mass destruction. As is well known, air warfare was created in the twentieth century as an instrument of state terror to entirely neutralize or destroy "vital centers" - that is, cities, thereby obliterating the difference between combatants and non-combatants in war. (A brief history of air warfare doctrine is posted on IEER's website.) Nuclear weapons extended the terror of conventional explosive bombing and fire bombing to a new dimension. But September 11, 2001 has nonetheless created a dreadful watershed in world history. The preponderance of evidence indicates that a non-state party, a terrorist network, has now used civilian aircraft as weapons of mass destruction to kill thousands.

The possibility that terrorists may create destruction on a vast scale has until now been postulated in studies and hinted at by many actual acts of terrorism such as the 1995 Oklahoma City bombing of the Alfred P. Murrah Federal Building, the 1993 bombing of the World Trade Center, and the 1995 chemical attack on a Tokyo subway. But the enormous scale and coordination of the assault, the choice of targets, the years of preparation, and the results of the September 11, 2001 attack mean that what was once largely hypothetical has moved into the column of grim reality.

The risk of continued terrorist attack remains, according to the US government. Retributive violence would add to the risks of continued terrorism, and it may also add to the risk of escalation to the use of nuclear, chemical, or biological weapons by a terrorist group. We do not know if some non-state groups already have nuclear materials. And we do not know how much they might have, if they do. Specifically, instability and conflict in Pakistan, a nuclear-armed state, over cooperation with US military actions might have unpredictable consequences.

It is imperative that we try to persuade the US government against a policy of violence and for a process that will lead to capture of the suspects and a trial. Moreover, if eradication of terrorism is the overall goal, a trial of the suspected plotters and financiers would reveal more about how terror networks are organized and maintained than a violent elimination of the suspects. The Nuremberg trials not only brought many of the perpetrators of the Holocaust to justice but also revealed great detail about how it was organized and implemented. They also led to important advances in international law. A trial in relation to the September 11 attacks would also show the world the best side of the traditions of the United States: the struggle for the rule of law and justice that motivated the American constitution, which has inspired not only generations of Americans but also freedom fighters worldwide.

But we need more than a trial. We need a process will lead to a progressive diminution of the conflicts and hatreds that lead up to acts of terror and indiscriminate killing. It is widely recognized that they are rooted in the terrible injustices and inequities that characterize our world. Reducing violence requires a reduction in militarism and repression by states and a systematic reduction of the great inequities in the world, so that people can have hope instead of despair. One analysis and discussion of the world economic and military structure as a kind of global apartheid (with some important differences) can be found in a July 9, 2001 article in *The Nation* by Salih Booker and William Minter. Another can be found in my book, *From Global Capitalism to Economic Justice*, (Apex Press, 1992, reprinted in 1996), along with a discussion of possible approaches to reduce global inequity and violence.

Given the level, scale and geographical spread of inequity, injustice, and anger in the world, it is likely that violent retribution by the United States would lead to global disunity and more conflict. It would increase the likelihood of more terrorist attacks, possibly more devastating ones. Such a prospect would be made more likely if US retribution produces large-scale civilian casualties.

Oil is and has been, through much of the twentieth century, one of the central aspects to the violent tangle of Middle Eastern, Central Asian, US, and world politics. The Japanese attack on Pearl Harbor came after the US imposed an oil embargo to prevent Japan from getting access to and eventual control of Indonesian oil, which belonged neither to Japan, nor to the United States, nor to the Dutch colonialists who then ruled Indonesia. As another example, the CIA-supported overthrow of an elected government in Iran in 1953 (in reaction to nationalization of the Iranian oil industry) and its replacement by the Shah of Iran led to two and a half decades of repression in which substantial dissent was only possible in the mosques. The process was central to the dynamic that led up to the 1979 Islamic revolution in Iran. For an excellent history of oil politics, see Daniel Yergin, *The Prize: The Epic Quest for Oil, Money and Power*, (New York: Simon and Schuster, 1991). For a fine, recent analysis of Central Asian oil resources and US policy see Michael Klare, *Resource Wars: The New Landscape of Global Conflict*, (New York: Metropolitan Books, 2001).

Much US policy in the Middle East makes for alliances with undemocratic regimes, including the one in Saudi Arabia, where, as in Afghanistan, no freedom of religion is allowed. That the Saudi Islamic government has allowed the stationing of US troops in Saudi Arabia, which has the two places most sacred to Muslims as well as the largest oil reserves in the world, has been in the center of the anger of some Islamic militants of the region. (See for instance a TV interview with Osama bin Laden partly conducted by ABC news correspondent John Miller in 1998. See also Mary Ann Weaver's article on Osama bin Laden in the *New Yorker* and John K. Cooley, *Unholy Wars: Afghanistan, America and International Terrorism*, Second Edition, (London, Pluto Press, 2000).) And as is increasingly recognized, those angry militants largely come from the phase of US policy that funded and trained them in the 1980s to oust the Soviet military from Afghanistan. Later, the Taliban was partly funded by Saudi Arabia until the 1998 bombings of the US embassies in Kenya and Tanzania. For a brief history of the Taliban, see Ahmed Rashid, "The Taliban: Exporting Extremism," *Foreign Affairs*, November/December 1999, pp. 22-35).

If retribution and violence are the wrong answers, how can the people of the world work together to pursue justice and increased security? Active, non-violent resistance to evil that goes to the root of the problem in a manner that everyone could participate was the

Illustration by Bindia Thapar

hallmark of the Gandhian struggle for India's independence, known as Satyagraha, as it was of the US civil rights movement, and the anti-apartheid struggle in South Africa. Making salt, making cloth, and desegregating lunch counters and buses were everyday acts that mobilized millions.

The Gandhian struggle in India had a part of its inspiration in US history-in the acts of Henry David Thoreau in the mid-nineteenth century to resist an unjust war and slavery. The civil rights struggle led by Martin Luther King, inspired in part by Gandhi's example, was non-violent resistance to injustice returning to the United States. This rich history can perhaps provide us with the inspiration we need in these grim and sad days to find ways to resist the violence both from weapons of mass destruction but also from injustice and exploitation that has come to characterize global society. More than five hundred million children have died needless deaths from starvation, lack of clean water, and lack of elementary medical care since World War II. At the same time, the wealthiest 400 people control more wealth than the poorest two billion. Maintenance of such inequalities requires a vast and global repressive machinery that has led to many valiant struggles for justice, but also bred hopelessness, anger, and hate.

October 2 is Gandhi's birthday. Perhaps it can be a day when we can all reflect on what we might do individually, in our communities, and on a global scale to resist militarism and violence, whether it comes from non-state groups or from states and to help create security, peace and justice.

For instance, one way in which those of us who live in the West and consume more than our fair share of fossil fuels can resist the cynical and militarist politics of oil to reduce our petroleum consumption as much as we can. A 25 percent reduction in oil consumption in the wealthy countries would amount to about 10 million barrels a day-more than the production of Saudi Arabia, which is the world's largest oil exporter. That could change the face of oil politics. While we cannot completely eliminate the use of oil in short and medium term-it would cause immense economic dislocation and suffering-significant voluntary reduction of oil consumption as well as sensible policies to that same end could help create a direction of greater equity, security, and environmental sanity. The soldiers who may be sent to fight in the desert sands, or those who are already there, with oil as a prime objective, would breathe easier too. (For an analysis of the proposed Bush administration energy policy and for IEER's energy policy recommendations see *Science for Democratic Action*, vol. 9 number 4, August 2001). Another idea that has been put forth is to send food to the villages of Afghanistan instead of bombs. That act of love might create cooperation from the heart that may increase the chance that there will be a trial instead of cycles of escalating violence. The official rhetoric in Washington makes it seem unlikely that the US government would, at this stage, take actions friendly to the people of Afghanistan-indeed it is in the contrary direction.

How people to people diplomacy might be conducted around the world to create a direction of peace at a time when the talk of war is so loud is a major challenge, to say the least. But Nelson Mandela, the African National Congress, and the people of South Africa joined by people all over the world used Gandhi as an inspiration to get rid of apartheid in South Africa. We now need a bigger struggle that taps into the same roots to get rid of global apartheid.

It will take the cooperation of organizations and people of goodwill around the world to rise to the challenge. We might begin this October 2 by gathering in our communities to remember those who died in a common global disaster and to ponder what we might do together across national boundaries that would honor the global nature of the tragedy and prevent its repetition. At meetings around the world on that date, we might gather to consider the questions of justice and of finding a path away from global apartheid, global violence and militarism, whether by states or terrorist groups, and towards global democracy, justice, equity, and friendship.

Arjun Makhijani is based at the Institute for Energy and Environmental Research (IEER), 2104 Stevens Ave. South, Minneapolis, MN 55404 USA. E-Mail: ieer@ieer.org

Illustration by Bindia Thapar

Nothing to Say to You

Sarveshwar Dayal Saxena

If a fire raged
in one room of your house
Could you sleep in the next room?

If a dead body lay
in one room of your house
Could you sing in the next room?

If corpses lay rotting
in one room of your house
Could you pray in the next room?

If yes,
then I have nothing
Nothing at all to say to you.

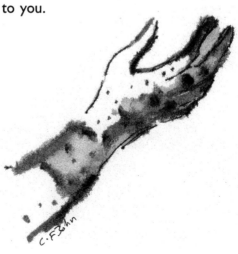

English Translation by Bindia Thapar. Illustration by C F John

This cloud has no silver lining

Say NO to Nuclear War!

Words and Illustration by Bindia Thapar

America's Unlimited War

Rahul Mahajan and Robert Jensen

For more than a week everyone has been saying that our world changed on Sept. 11.

In fact, it was on Sept. 20 that the world changed, the day that George W. Bush spoke to the nation and announced the American jihad.

"Every nation in every region now has a decision to make," he said. "Either you are with us, or you are with the terrorists." Independent policy, middle ground – it appears these are concepts of the old world.

The Taliban, he said, must "hand over every terrorist and every person in their support structure." Punishment only for the guilty – another irrelevant concept. What is a support structure? That's a question for those who don't understand the new war.

"They will hand over the terrorists or they will share in their fate." Collective punishment is part of the new world order.

Bush has said repeatedly that this isn't about a clash of religions. But, he told us, "Freedom and fear, justice and cruelty, have always been at war, and we know that God is not neutral between them."

God has signed on with us, and so difficult questions need not be asked. We need have no qualms about a campaign to – in the words of the secretary of defence – "drain the swamp," borrowing on an old counterinsurgency term that translates into killing civilians to deprive targeted groups of their "cover."

The goal of this new campaign is "Infinite Justice." The Pentagon has retracted that name, with its overtones of Christian fundamentalism, in deference to the sentiments of Muslims. But it cannot retract the uneasy feeling the phrase leaves us with, for the Pentagon planners are not speaking of justice spread infinitely throughout the world.

Instead, it is "justice" ad infinitum – to the end. The war of the 21st century begins now.

It is justice by the sword. It ends in victory not peace, and Bush has made it clear that the sword will be unsheathed for a long time to come.

It did not have to be this way. Even after the provocation of such a brutal and inhuman attack, the United States could have chosen the path of sanity. Bush could have said that 56 years of a national security state has done nothing to assure our security and has only endangered us.

He could have said that America's course of unilateralism, military aggression, and economic domination must be rethought.

He could have said that support for Israel's occupation of Palestine and for the brutal economic siege of Iraq should be rethought.

He could have said at least that there was no need to exacerbate risks at a time of great tension, that there was no need of a rash insistence that our demands "are not open to negotiation or discussion." He need not have threatened to use "every necessary weapon of war."

We stand at a juncture in history, a moment in which our course can be changed. We need political leaders who can see what a disaster past policies have been. We need people with vision, who can imagine what a just world would look like.

As Democrats and Republicans in Congress all showered with praise Bush's call for an unlimited war with unending enemies, never before has it been so clear that the existing political leadership of this country is bankrupt.

No one from any part of the political spectrum – left, right, or centre – or any walk of life – rich, poor, or middle class – can any longer afford the illusion that being a good citizen means supporting the status quo.

Bush wanted to galvanise a nation, and in a strange way he might have. As we watch leaders callously leverage the suffering of Americans into carte blanche for their jihad, we see how the world has changed for the worse.

There is nothing to do but face that reality – not cynically in despair, but realistically with hope and the understanding that we can change it for the better. In the spontaneous demonstrations of resistance that have sprung up the past few days, we may be seeing the seeds of that change. Ordinary Americans are beginning to see that we are connected more to Afghan peasants, in our shared vulnerability, than to any of the people with the fingers on the triggers – the terrorists or the man in the White House.

Radical change is not only possible, it has begun.

Rahul Mahajan serves on the National Board of Peace Action, USA. Robert Jensen is a professor of journalism at the University of Texas. Both are members of the Nowar Collective (www.nowarcollective.com).

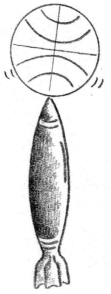

Illustration by Bindia Thapar

Illustration by C F John

Put Out No Flags

Katha Pollitt

My daughter, who goes to Stuyvesant High School only blocks from the World Trade Center, thinks we should fly an American flag out our window. Definitely not, I say: The flag stands for jingoism and vengeance and war. She tells me I'm wrong—the flag means standing together and honoring the dead and saying no to terrorism. In a way we're both right: The Stars and Stripes is the only available symbol right now. In New York City, it decorates taxicabs driven by Indians and Pakistanis, the impromptu memorials of candles and flowers that have sprung up in front of every firehouse, the chi-chi art galleries and boutiques of SoHo. It has to bear a wide range of meanings, from simple, dignified sorrow to the violent anti-Arab and anti-Muslim bigotry that has already resulted in murder, vandalism and arson around the country and harassment on New York City streets and campuses. It seems impossible to explain to a 13-year-old, for whom the war in Vietnam might as well be the War of Jen! kins's Ear, the connection between waving the flag and bombing ordinary people half a world away back to the proverbial stone age. I tell her she can buy a flag with her own money and fly it out her bedroom window, because that's hers, but the living room is off-limits.

There are no symbolic representations right now for the things the world really needs—equality and justice and humanity and solidarity and intelligence. The red flag is too bloodied by history; the peace sign is a retro fashion accessory. In much of the world, including parts of this country, the cross and crescent and Star of David are logos for nationalistic and sectarian hatred. Ann Coulter, fulminating in her syndicated column, called for carpet-bombing of any country where people "smiled" at news of the disaster: "We should invade their countries, kill their leaders, and convert them to Christianity." What is this, the Crusades? The Rev. Jerry Falwell issued a belated mealy-mouthed apology for his astonishing remarks immediately after the attacks, but does anyone doubt that he meant them? The disaster was God's judgment on secular America, he observed, as famously secular New Yorkers were rushing to volunteer to dig out survivors, to give blood, food, money, anything–it! was all the fault of "the pagans, and the abortionists, and the feminists, and the gays and the lesbians...the ACLU, People for the American Way." That's what the Taliban think too.

As I write, the war talk revolves around Afghanistan, home of the vicious Taliban and hideaway of Osama bin Laden. I've never been one to blame the United States for every bad thing that happens in the Third World, but it is a fact that our government supported militant Islamic fundamentalism in Afghanistan after the Soviet invasion in 1979. The mujahedeen were freedom fighters against Communism, backed by more than $3 billion in US aid–more money and expertise than for any other cause in CIA history–and hailed as heroes by tag-along journalists from Dan Rather to William T. Vollmann, who saw these lawless fanatics as manly primitives untainted by the West. (There's a story in here about the attraction Afghan hypermasculinity holds for desk-bound modern men. How lovely not to pay lip service to women's equality! It's cowboys and Indians, with harems thrown in.) And if, with the Soviets gone, the vying warlords turned against one another, raped and pillaged and murdered the civilian population and destroyed what still remained of normal Afghan life, who could have predicted that? These people! The Taliban, who rose out of this period of devastation, were boys, many of them orphans, from the wretched refugee camps of Pakistan, raised in the unnatural womanless hothouses of fundamentalist boarding schools. Even leaving aside their ignorance and provincialism and lack of modern skills, they could no more be expected to lead Afghanistan back to normalcy than an army made up of kids raised from birth in Romanian orphanages.

Feminists and human-rights groups have been sounding the alarm about the Taliban since they took over Afghanistan in 1996. That's why interested Americans know that Afghan women are forced to wear the total shroud of the burqa and are banned from work and from leaving their homes unless accompanied by a male relative; that girls are barred from school; and that the Taliban–far from being their nation's saviors, enforcing civic peace with their terrible swift Kalashnikovs–are just the latest oppressors of the miserable population. What has been the response of the West to this news? Unless you count the absurd infatuation of European intellectuals with the anti-Taliban Northern Alliance of fundamentalist warlords (here we go again!), not much.

What would happen if the West took seriously the forces in the Muslim world who call for education, social justice, women's rights, democracy, civil liberties and secularism? Why does our foreign policy underwrite the clerical fascist government of Saudi Arabia– and a host of nondemocratic regimes besides? What is the point of the continuing sanctions on Iraq, which have brought untold misery to ordinary people and awakened the most backward tendencies of Iraqi society while doing nothing to undermine Saddam Hussein? And why on earth are fundamentalist Jews from Brooklyn and Philadelphia allowed to turn Palestinians out of their homes on the West Bank? Because God gave them the land? Does any sane person really believe that?

Bombing Afghanistan to "fight terrorism" is to punish not the Taliban but the victims of the Taliban, the people we should be supporting. At the same time, war would reinforce the worst elements in our own society–the flag-wavers and bigots and militarists. It's heartening that there have been peace vigils and rallies in many cities, and antiwar actions are planned in Washington, DC, for September 29-30, but look what even the threat of war has already done to Congress, where only a single representative, Barbara Lee, Democrat from California, voted against giving the President virtual carte blanche.

A friend has taken to wearing her rusty old women's Pentagon Action buttons–at least they have a picture of the globe on them. The globe, not the flag, is the symbol that's wanted now.

Katha Politt is the editor of America's pre-eminent weekly, Nation. *This piece appeared in the weekly on September 18, 2001.*

God stands divided
by Temple, Mosque
And Church

Earth is divided, divided our oceans
Stop dividing humanity,
We urge

Original poem in Hindi by Vinay Mahajan. English translation by Kamla Bhasin.
Illustration by Rajasthan Kisan Sanghatana.

To My Seven-Year-Old

Kavita Ramdas

How do I explain to my seven-year-old daughter, Mira, that her last name, Ahmad, was the first or last name of six of the men listed as "hijackers"?

How do I explain to Mira that Pakistan, her father Zuli's home country, is not a place where the "bad guys" are from?

How do I explain that there are moments when Zuli and I fear that this will lead to an all out world war that will begin in our part of the world, where two countries (India, which is my birthplace, and Pakistan) now have nuclear weapons?

How do I explain that the use of terror and violence does not justify further violence, using, of course, a kid-appropriate example?

How can I explain feeling suddenly afraid that other kids will make fun of my kid because she is "foreign, or Muslim, or Pakistani", even here in safe, liberal, tolerant Palo Alto?

How do I explain wanting to pick her up and put her between Zuli and me on our bed every night, after all the effort we've made to encourage her to sleep on her own?

How do I explain the tears that come to my eyes for no reason in the middle of a sentence? What do I say when Zuli's sister calls from Pakistan to say the airports have been closed for three days and people are preparing for US troops to move in?

So instead of explaining, Zuli and I are holding onto the common, dear things that make our lives liveable. We go to soccer practice, where an Iranian kid and a Korean kid and a French kid and a Indo/Pakistani kid and a Jewish kid and an African American kid kick a ball on a field. And where parents whose eyes are full of tears and throats are choked with fear put on brave smiles and coach them just like it was any other day.

We are holding on to the many friends who have called or stopped by our home to say that they are worried for our families in Pakistan and India. We are holding on to the kindness of total strangers who come up to me to express their horror at the Indian who was killed in Arizona and the Pakistani who died in Texas.

These things demonstrate the basic decency and humanity that give America its great strength, it's belief in diversity, and its courage to let a range of perspectives be expressed even at a time of mourning. We can hold on to those things and so can our kids.

Kavita N. Ramdas is the President of the Global Fund For Women.

Illustration by Bindia Thapar

All of a Sudden Our Names Have Become Our Liability

A. H. Jaffor Ullah

In every sort of danger, there are various ways of winning through, if one is ready to do and say anything whatever."

Socrates

On September 11, 2001, the day America was under siege in morning hours, CBS anchorman Dan Rather was chatting with Fouad Ajami, a John Hopkins University professor, in the live broadcast from CBS's New York City studio over the day's unprecedented events. Professor Ajami is a noted scholar on Islamic world. Whenever Arab world is implicated with anything pros or cons, Professor Ajami is summoned to the CBS studio. Tuesday, September 12 was no different. The erudite professor was adamant when he said that if either Osama bin Laden or any Islamic terrorist groups from Middle East were implicated in this crime against humanity, there will be massive repercussions against Muslim Americans for sure. CBS's veteran anchorperson Dan Rather immediately sensed the implication of Prof. Ajami's statement; he was quick to remind the viewers that overwhelming Muslims living in America have nothing to do with terrorism; therefore, we should not stereotype the Muslim people with terrorism. It is comforting to know that CBS's Dan Rather would go an extra mile to warn the viewers that we should not equate Muslim folks living in America with terrorism.

In spite of all the forewarning given to the viewers in all the news channels, this scribe has serious doubts that every one in the West will pay heed to TV sages such as Dan Rather, Tom Brokaw, or anyone like them. Thus, Muslims living in the West or for that matter, Caucasian Asian people with dark skin should brace for tough time ahead. Professor Ajami's prediction came true sooner than one could think. Of course, we all know that on February 26, 1993, some Muslim terrorists bombed the World Trade Centre and in the aftermath of that bombing Arab Muslims in America had to endure a deluge of verbal insults and humiliation. But this time, in the wake of Black Tuesday's demolition of WTC's Twin Tower and parts of Pentagon Building by suspected Arab terrorists the situation is one-hundred times more grievous than the past one. Therefore, the Muslim communities in America and even in Europe are bracing for bad times ahead.

Barely two days after the suicidal terrorists' carnage we heard the news in the radio (CNN) that Muslim people became the object of ridicule and derisiveness. In Dallas, a mosque took some bullets; whereas in Chicago, an Arab business was hit by Molotov Cocktail. Also, elsewhere in America a Pakistani woman dressed in ethnic garb was about to be run over by an irate driver. Because of all these incidents happening in four corners of America, we have received e-mails from various sources in which specific instructions were given how to avoid unpleasant circumstances. Here in America not only the people from Middle-Eastern background were singled out for retaliatory action, but immigrants from South Asia also were receiving epithets and physical threats.

In New York City, where emotions are running high, turban-clad Sikhs were singled out mistakenly as Arabs. Some of those folks also received physical threats. Here in Louisiana, a schoolteacher asked my spouse point blank whether her name is an Islamic one. Although there was no threat associated with such questioning, but the experience could be bone chilling.

Just 72 hours after the demolition of skyscrapers in New York City, the FBI has released the name of 18 suspected terrorists who engineered the vile attack. Here I reproduce the names of these terrorists. The suspected hijackers aboard American Airlines Flight 11, which hit the north tower of the World Trade Centre, were: 1. Walid Al Shehri; 2. Wail Alsheri aka Waleed Alsheri; 3. Mohammad Atta; 4. Aabdul Alomari; 5. Satam Sugami. Aboard United Airlines Flight 175, which hit the south tower of the World Trade Centre, the suspected hijackers were: 6. Marawn Alshehhi; 7. Fayez Ahmed; 8. Mohald Alshehri, 9. Hamza Al Ghamdi; 10. Ahmed Al Ghamdi.

Those believed to be the hijackers aboard American Airlines Flight 77, which hit the Pentagon, were: 11. Khalid Almihdhar; 12. Majed Moqued; 13. Nawaf Al Hazmi; 14. Salem Al Hazmi. The suspected hijackers aboard United Airlines Flight 93, which crashed in rural Pennsylvania, were: 15. Ahmed Al Haznawi; 16. Ahmed Alnami; 17. Ziad Jarrah; 18. Saeed Alghamdi.

There is a reason for listing those names of the suspected terrorists. One can easily see that most of those suspected terrorists have Arabic names. Muslim people irrespective of where they come from have names such as Abdul, Mohammed, Ahmed, Saeed, Khaild, etc. The Americans who have very little contact with the outside world (believe me, there are plenty of them everywhere) may have got the impression that Arabic sounding names belong to terrorists and as such people having such names in their communities may have something to do with terrorism. This is what is called "guilt by association." This is a real nightmare for many Asian immigrants who live in urban areas known to be ethnic neighbourhood.

In the aftermath of Black Tuesday, September 11, 2001, we find ourselves very vulnerable and this is all because of the action of a handful Arab terrorists. Suddenly, our Arabic sounding names have become our greatest liability. Quite a few South Asian Muslims have instructed their children who attend schools not to associate their names with Arabs. Suddenly, our South Asian identity has taken a different meaning. Mind you, not too long ago, some of our folks from Bangladesh used to relish on our Middle-Eastern roots via Islam, our main religion in our motherland. All that is changing very fast. Some new parents are making some compromise by picking names such as Adam, Daniel, Sarah, Miriam to camouflage their Muslim identity. Not a bad trick, may I add? On the extreme side, though, some folks whom I have talked have indicated that changing the names is a distinct possibility. Some have started thinking in that direction. On Friday, September 14, 2001, I saw a write-up in News From Bangladesh, an Internet newspaper for expatriates, in which a writer by the name Jahed Ahmed has publicly changed his name to Ray Jahed Akash. It is an interesting name having three components each comprising of a Western, Arabic, and Indic names. Therefore, it will be easy for Jahed Ahmed to be known as Ray. Thereby, he may be excluded from any future wrath directed to folks with unusual Middle-Eastern name.

It is too early to say whether Jahed Ahmed has started a new trend or not. However, it is for sure that tens and thousands of people living in the West who have Arabic names are now thinking seriously about the implications of having an Arabic name in the wake of devastating terrorists' attack in American soil. Suddenly, we are facing the reality that our very names that were given to us by our parents at birth have become our greatest liability.

A.H. Jaffor Ullah, a scientist, writes from New Orleans, USA.

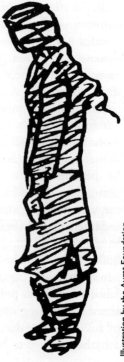

Illustration by the Aurat Foundation

Will Pakistan Jump to US Demands?

Tariq Ali

On a trip to Pakistan a few years ago I was talking to an ex-General about the militant Islamist groups in the region. I asked him why these people, who had happily accepted funds and weapons from the United States throughout the Cold War, had become violently anti-American overnight. He explained that they were not alone. Many Pakistan officers who had served the US loyally from 1951 onwards felt humiliated by Washington's indifference.

'Pakistan was the condom the Americans needed to enter Afghanistan', he said. 'We've served our purpose and they think we can be just flushed down the toilet.' The old condom is being fished out for use once again, but will it work? The new 'coalition against terrorism' needs the services of the Pakistan Army, but General Musharraf will have to be extremely cautious. An over-commitment to Washington could lead to a civil war in Pakistan and split the Armed Forces. A great deal has changed over the last two decades, but the ironies of history continue to multiply.

In Pakistan itself, Islamism derived its strength from state patronage rather than popular support. The ascendancy of religious fundamentalism is the legacy of a previous military dictator, General Zia-ul-Haq who received solid backing from Washington and London throughout his 11 years as dictator.

It was during his rule (1977-89) that a network of *madrassahs* (religious boarding schools), funded by the Saudi regime, were created.

The children, who were later sent to fight as Mujahedeen in Afghanistan, were taught to banish all doubt. The only truth was divine truth. Anyone who rebelled against the imam rebelled against

Allah. The madrassahs had only one aim: the production of deracinated fanatics in the name of a bleak Islamic cosmpolitanism. The primers taught that the Urdu letter jeem stood for 'jihad'; tay for 'tope'(cannon), kaaf for Kalashnikov and khay for 'khoon' (blood).

2500 madrassahs produced a crop of 225,000 fanatics ready to kill and die for their faith when asked to do so by their religious leaders despatched across the border by the Pakistan Army, they were hurled into battle against other Muslims they were told were not true Muslims. The Taliban creed is an ultra-sectarian strain, inspired by the Wahhabi sect that rules Saudi Arabia. The severity of the Afghan mullahs has been denounced by Sunni clerics at al-Azhar in Cairo and Shi-ite theologians in Qom as a disgrace to the Prophet.

The Taliban could not, however, have captured Kabul on their own via an excess of religious zeal. They were armed and commanded by 'volunteers' from the Pakistan Army. If Islamabad decided to pull the plug, the Taliban could be dislodged, but not without serious problems. The victory in Kabul counts as the Pakistani Army's only triumph. To this day, the former US Secretary of State, Zbigniew Brezinski remains recalcitrant: 'What was more important in the world view of history?' he asks with more than a touch of irritation, 'the Taliban or the fall of the Soviet Empire? A few stirred-up Muslims or the liberation of Central Europe and the end of the Cold War?'

If Hollywood rules necessitate a short, sharp war against the new enemy, the American Caesar would be best-advised not to insist on Pakistani legions. The consequences could be dire: a brutal and vicious civil war creating more bitterness and encouraging more acts of individual terrorism. Islamabad will do everything to prevent a military expedition to Afghanistan. For one thing there are Pakistani soldiers, pilots and officers present in Kabul, Bagram and other bases. What will be their orders this time and will they obey them? Much more likely is that Osama Bin Laden will be sacrificed in the interests of the greater cause and his body dead or alive will be handed over to his former employers in Washington. But will that be enough?

The only real solution is a political one. It requires removing the causes that create the discontent. It is despair that feeds fanaticism and it is a result of Washington's policies in the Middle East and elsewhere. The orthodox casuistry among loyal factotums, columnists and courtiers of the Washington regime is symbolised by Tony Blair's Personal Assistant for Foreign Affairs, ex-diplomat Robert Cooper, who writes quite openly: 'We need to get used to the idea of double standards'.

The underlying maxim of this cynicism is: we will punish the crimes of our enemies and reward the crimes of our friends. Isn't that at least preferable to universal impunity? To this the answer is simple: 'punishment' along these lines does not reduce but breeds criminality, by those who wield it. The Gulf and Balkan Wars were copy-book examples of the moral blank cheque of a selective vigilantism. Israel can defy UN resolutions with impunity, India can tyrannise Kashmir, Russia can destroy Groszny, but it is Iraq which has to be punished and it is the Palestinians who continue to suffer.

Cooper continues: 'Advice to post-modern states: accept that intervention in the pre-modern is going to be a fact of life. Such interventions may not solve problems, but they may salve the conscience. And they are not necessarily the worse for that' Try explaining that to the survivors in New York and Washington.

The United States is whipping itself into a frenzy. Its ideologues talk of this as an attack on 'civilisation', but what kind of civilisation is it that thinks in terms of blood-revenge. For the last sixty years and more the United States has toppled democrat leaders, bombed countries in three continents, used nuclear weapons against Japanese civilians, but never knew what it felt like to have your own cities under attack. Now they know.

To the victims of the attack and their relatives one can offer our deep sympathy as one does to people who the US government has victimised. But to accept that somehow an American life is worth more than that of a Rwandan, a Yugoslav, a Vietnamese, a Korean, a Japanese, a Palestinian...that is unacceptable.

Tariq Ali is a London-based Pakistani journalist.

My eyes are moist
With the tears of all eyes

The pain of all hearts
Is mine.

Original Poem in Urdu by Firaq Gorakhpuri. English translation by Kamla Bhasin. Illustration by Rajasthan Kisan Sanghatana.

A View from the Ground

Rina Saeed Khan

I am sitting here in Islamabad. surrounded by the travelling media circus (that really is the only way to describe them). The performers are not just the usual suspects: CNN, BBC, CBS, Fox, Star, Sky etc. but representatives from all the major European, Japanese and Arab channels. They tell me this is the biggest story since WW II - and unfortunately, the focus is on Pakistan and the Taliban.

I suppose I should write a proper account of all that I have experienced since I arrived here last Saturday. But for now, here's a summary.

I flew into Islamabad with the BBC Newsnight team (the programme comes on every week-night on BBC2). Since then, I have gone up and down the majestic Khyber Pass (near the Afghanistan border), crossed the River Kabul on a rickety wooden boat, visited over-crowded Afghan refugee camps that stretch for miles, tried to bluff my way into the Taliban Embassy in Islamabad, been harassed by moronic Pakistani intelligence, been admonished by a bearded/turbaned fundo from the Movement for Jihad, and actually been impressed by an erudite Mullah who pointed out that to a large extent, the media is to blame for this debacle. "One hour after the blast the media began blaming Osama bin Laden. and without evidence, the American government declared him the enemy".

These views are not just held by the mullahs or the Taliban (who are also asking for proof in order to hand over Osama bin Laden) - wherever we have gone and whoever we have met here in Pakistan (scores of journalists, analysts, govt. officials and ordinary citizens of this country), the same question keeps recurring: "What evidence is there to prove that Osama bin Laden is responsible for the WTC bombing? And why should the people of Afghanistan have to suffer for an act they did not even commit?"

We have no answer to give to them except that the Americans are angry and they want someone to pay for what happened in New York and Washington. So, a devastated, drought-stricken nation it will have to be - a country already bombed into the stone-age and ruled by psychotic soldiers. Who exactly are the Taliban? They are the orphans of the Cold War, whose fathers bled Communist Russia for 10 years, allowing the Americans to become the world's only superpower. The holy warriors have now been turned into evil terrorists. Yesterday the Taliban, under enormous pressure from Pakistan, announced that they have "asked Osama to leave voluntarily" - the Americans have responded by saying that is "unacceptable". It looks like we are headed for war. the Americans are determined to retaliate.

The media, smelling blood, is hyping itself up for the strikes - sadly, no one is asking the most crucial question: WHY? As Robert Fisk writes, "Every effort will be made in the coming days to switch off the 'why' question and concentrate on the who, what and how. CNN and most of the world's media have already obeyed this essential new war rule".

I don't know what will happen in the next few days. but I do know that once the attack begins, there will be a huge backlash that will not just affect Pakistan, but the entire region. Bush keeps saying "Make no mistake" - unfortunately, I think he's about to make the biggest mistake of the century. As this retired General, who has close links with the Afghan people, told me "This is the wrong people, the wrong country and the wrong time - the Americans have no idea what they are about to unleash". In the words of Robert Fisk, "Retaliation leads to retaliation and more retaliation. War without end."

I'm sorry for being so depressing. but maybe all this craziness has to happen before some sort of sanity prevails in the world.

Rina Saeed Khan, formerly of the weekly The Friday Times *of Pakistan, is now a freelance journalist stringing for the* BBC Newsnight *team.*

Cloud Over New York?

Indira Jaising

Not that it has not been said before, but I cannot help comparing the cloud over New York with the cloud over Bhopal on the night of 2/3 December 1984, when as many people if not more died, or were injured in a man-made disaster. I do not see any essential difference between the two events, though separated in time and space. The so-called accident in Bhopal, was as much born of human will and agency, as the demolition of the World Trade Towers. In Bhopal, the technology of death and destruction was the consequence of gross criminal neglect, controlled by the US corporation, Union Carbide, which today, like its terrorist counterpart, has lost its original identity and metamorphosised into other headless entities. Today, it is President Bush who says "Wanted Osama bin Laden, dead or alive" Yesterday, it was Warren Anderson, who fled like a rat from this country to avoid standing trial on charges of murder, and criminal negligence, fled to the safe haven of the United States of America. And I seem to remember the victims of the Bhopal tragedy saying similar things, sticking posters of Warren Anderson in the streets of Bhopal with the slogan, "wanted dead or alive". Today, it is President Bush who says, "we are in hot pursuit" Yesterday, it was Indians who were saying, "we are in pursuit of Warren Anderson" But there is one major difference, India did not declare the act of industrial terrorism an act of war, the USA has, and India did not retaliate with the threat of war against the USA or Union Carbide, as the USA does threaten in Afghanistan. India tamely asked for extradition.

Perhaps the difference lies in the fact that the victims of the Bhopal tragedy do not have the same extra-territorial jurisdiction over terrorists of a different country that a powerful President Bush has.

There are so many other comparisons that come to mind. Images of people in the streets of New York carrying pictures of their loved ones remind one of the mothers of Argentina and other Latin American countries who carried pictures of their loved ones who had "disappeared" in military regimes supported by the USA. There is a sameness about language as well. In the one case the word" disappeared" and in the other case the word "missing" are both euphemisms for death, unnatural death. The word " disappeared" has come to acquire a legal meaning in the language of human rights instruments, it means death due to abduction and torture, the body never being found. The word "missing" forever has a different meaning in legal literature, unaccounted for deaths. So what is it then ? Does disaster have a way of reproducing itself after a gestation period? Can the causes of disasters occurring in different times and spaces be linked in some logical manner, a logic which the world refuses to see? Are the two disasters, the one in Bhopal and the one in New York so unlinked after all? I think not. Both were born in the same womb, in the United States of America, which again, is not a place but a concept. Bhopal and New York both teach us about the interconnectedness of human life and death. Humanity cannot insure itself against itself.

Is there also a sameness about forms of protest? The mute grief of the relatives of the "missing" is no different from silent marches of the mothers of the 'disappeared". Their sameness lies in their helplessness.

Silence is the ultimate weapon of the oppressed, it is the road to justice and peace. . . That there is sameness about human suffering was poignantly brought out by hundreds of people willing to volunteer blood. Human blood is human blood, regardless of the nationality or colour of the person donating it, and regardless of the colour of the person to whom it is donated. We all wrote to friends enquiring if they were all right. But at a time like this, every injured human being is a friend. And whether innocent people in Afghanistan or New York die, their suffering is no different. The happenings in New York teach us about the sameness of suffering and of vulnerabilities, against which all the wealth in the world provides no insurance.

Indira Jaising, is a lawyer, a feminist and a human rights activist. She edits From the Lawyers Collective, *a monthly magazine about law and social justice.*

Solidarity Against All Forms of Terrorism

Vandana Shiva

18th September was the day for solidarity with victims of the September 11th terrorist attack on the U.S.

I joined the millions to observe two minutes silence at 10:30 a.m. for those who lost their lives in the assault on the World Trade Centre and the Pentagon.

But I also thought of the millions who are victims of other terrorist actions and other forms of violence. And I renewed my commitment to resist violence in all its forms.

At 10:30 a.m. on 18th September, I was with Laxmi, Raibari, Suranam in Jhodia Sahi village in Kashipur district in Orissa. Laxmi's husband Ghabi Jhodia was among the 20 tribals who have recently died of starvation.

In the same village Subarna Jhodia had also died. Later we met Singari in Bilamal village who has lost her husband Sadha, elder son Surat, younger son Paila and daughter- in-law Sulami.

The deliberate denial of food to the hungry is at the core of the World Bank Structural Adjustment programmes. Dismantling the Public Distribution System (PDS) was a World Bank conditionality.

It was justified on grounds of reducing expenditure. But the food subsidy budget has exploded from Rs. 2,800 crore in 1991 to Rs. 14,000 crore in 2001. More money is being spent to store grain because the Bank required that food subsidies be withdrawn. This led to increase in food prices, lowering of purchase from PDS and hence build up of stocks. The food security of the nation is collapsing.

While observing 2 minutes silence in the midst of tribal families who are victims of starvation even while 60 million tonnes are rotting in the godowns, I could not help but think of economic policies which push people into poverty and starvation as a form of terrorism.

Starvation deaths in Maharashtra, Rajasthan, Orissa are a symptom of the breakdown of our food systems. Kashipur was gifted with abundance of nature. Starvation does not belong here. It is the result of waves of violence against nature and the tribal communities. It is a result of a brutal state ever present to snatch the resources of the tribals for industry and private corporations, but totally absent in providing welfare and security to the dispossessed tribals.

The starvation deaths in Kashipur and other regions are a result of the ecological plunder of the resources of the region, the dismantling of the food, security system under economic reform policies and the impact of climate change which caused two years of crop failure due to drought and this year's crop failure due to excessive and unseasonal rain.

Twenty years ago, the pulp and paper industry raped the forests of Kashipur. Today the herbs stand naked, and the paper mills are bringing Eucalyptus from neighbouring Andhra Pradesh.

The terrorism of the pulp industry has already left the region devastated. Now the giant mining companies - Hydro of Norway, Alcan of Canada, Indico, Balco/Sterlite of India have unleashed a new wave of terror. They are eyeing the bauxite in the majestic hills of Kashipur. Bauxite is used for aluminium – aluminium that will go to make Coca Cola cans and fighter planes.

Imagine each mountain to be a World Trade Centre built by nature over millennia. Think of how many tragedies bigger than what the world experienced on Sep 11th are taking place to provide raw material for insatiable industry and markets. We stopped the ecological terrorism of the mining industry in my home - the Doon Valley - in 1983. The Supreme Court closed the mines, and ruled that commerce that threatens life must be stopped. But our ecological victories of the 1980s were undone with the environmental deregulation accompanying globalisation policies.

Mining has been "liberalised" and corporations are rushing to findminerals wherever they can. The Aluminium companies want the homelands of the Kashipur tribals.

But triabls of Kashipur refuse to leave their homes. They are defending the land and earth - through a non-violent resistance movement — the movement for the Protection of Nature and People". As Mukta Jhodia, an elderly woman leader of the movement said at a rally on 18th in Kashipur, "The earth is our mother. We are born of her. We are her children. The mining companies cannot force us to leave our land. This land was given to us by God and creation, not by the government. The government has no right to snatch our land from us."

This forced apportion of resources from people too is a form of terrorism - corporate terrorism.

I had gone to offer solidarity to victims of this corporate terrorism which was not only threatening to rob 200 villages of their survival base but had already robbed off their lives when they were shot and killed on 16th December 2000 by the police.

Abhilash was one of the victims killed in the police firing. His wife Subarna Jhodia was expecting a baby when he was shot. When I went to meet her in her village Maikanch, she was sitting on the doorstep of her hut with the baby girl who was born after the father was brutally killed. I asked her what she had named her child, she asked me to give her daughter a name. I named her Shakti - to embody power in peaceful form — to carry in her the 'Shakti' her father and his tribal colleagues have displayed over a decade of resistance against the terrorism of mining companies and a police state and one combined shakti to fight all forms of terrorism.

50 million triabls who have been flooded out of their homes by dams over the past 4 decades were also victims of terrorism - they have faced the terror of technology and destructive development.

For the 30,000 thousand people who died in the Orissa Supercyclone, and the millions who will die when flood and drought and cyclones become more severe because of climate change and fossil fuel pollution, President Bush is an ecological terrorist because he refuses to sign the Kyoto protocol.

And the WTO was named the World Terrorist Organisation by citizens in Seattle because its rules are denying millions the right to life and livelihood.

The tragedy of September 11 provides us with an opportunity to stop all forms of terrorism — militaristic, technological, economic, political. Terrorism will not be stopped by militarised minds which create insecurity and fear and hence breed terrorism. The present "war against terrorism" will create a vicious cycle of violence. It will not create peace and security. We are already witnessing a xenophobic wave sweeping across the U.S., with Indians, Asians and Arabs being attacked and killed. We are seeing fundamentalists of every hue emboldened by the mood for `revenge'.

Terrorism can only be stopped by cultures of peace, democracy, andpeople's security. It is wrong to define the post September 11th world as a war between "civilisation and barbarianism" or "democracy and terrorism". It is a war between two forms of terrorism which are mirror images of each other's mindsets - mindsets that can only conceive of monocultures and must erase diversity, the very pre-condition for peace. They share the dominant culture of violence. They used the same weapons and the same technologies. In terms of the preference for violence and use of terror, both sides are clones of each other. And their victims are innocent people everywhere.

The real conflict is between citizens across the world longing to live in peace and security and forces of violence and terror - denying them peace and security.

The tribals in Jhodia Sahi had lit a lamp for me at the village shrine - a small stone. These tribal shrines are insignificant when one measures them in physical terms against the twin towers of the World Trade Centre. But they are spiritually deeply significant because they embody a generous cosmology of peace - peace with the earth, peace between people, peace within people. This is the culture of peace we need to reclaim, and spread.

The whole world repeatedly watched the destruction of the World Trade Centre towers, but the destruction of millions of sacred shrines and homes and farms by forces of injustice, greed and globalisation go unnoticed.

As we remember the victims of Black Tuesday, let us also strengthen our solidarity with the millions of invisible victims of other forms of terrorism and violence which are threatening the very possibility of our future on this planet. We can turn this tragic brutal historical moment into building cultures of peace.

Vandana Shiva is the founder of the Research Foundation for Science, Technology and Ecology, New Delhi.

Counter-Terror will not Work

Praful Bidwai

Nothing since Hiroshima and Nagasaki has convulsed the world's conscience as powerfully as the butchery of innocent civilians in Tuesday's terror attacks in the US. However, the shock, agony and anger produced by these ghastly, wholly unconscionable, acts are now giving way to calls for revenge and retribution in America, and to loose talk of a new global alliance for "freedom and democracy" against "jehadi terrorism" in India.

American leaders insist on portraying these attacks as acts of "war". Many are deploying language reminiscent of Reagan's "Evil Empire", which would rationalise the unleashing of retribution with unlimited or maximum force in different parts of the world as America's "self-defence".

Colin Powell has gone so far as to threaten large-scale and long-term retaliation against terrorism-whether "it is legally correct or not".

And President Bush says he makes "no distinction" between "terrorists" and states that harbour them. A vengeful mindset has thus crystallised, which declares: if you're not with us, you're against us; we will pay the terrorists back in their own coin; force is the only language they understand...

Nothing could be more harmful than this mindset to the cause of democracy, freedom and pluralism-in name of which the retribution is being threatened. Equally, nothing could more badly undermine the cause of a just, plural, multilaterally balanced, rule-of-law-based world order than unilateral military action by Washington, whether undertaken formally under NATO auspices or not. Such action seems imminent. Yet, no power or state in the world is attempting to counsel restraint upon the US-neither the European

Union, nor Russia and China, nor even formerly strongly multilateralist states like India. The UN too has been passive.

Ironically, the world, or rather some more innocent civilians outside America's borders, could thus end up paying a high price through insensate violence and overwhelming use of force-just as New Yorkers tragically did.

The only way to prevent this is to immediately activate the Security Council and other multilateral instruments and mandate them to act in a way that balances the use of proportionate, moderate force under Chapter VII of the UN Charter, with a staunch defence of civil liberties. After the mess that NATO made through its unilateral intervention of the situation in the former Yugoslavia, especially Kosovo in 1999, there is a compelling reason for doing so. Yet, the prospect of this happening appears bleak.

Thus, we have the bizarre spectacle of a Cold War military alliance, which lost its very reason for existence a decade ago with the collapse of the Warsaw Pact, now invoking its "collective defence" Article 5–for the first time in half a century! The US as the dominant partner of this far-from-democratic military coalition-there has always been one finger, not two, on NATO's triggers-seems all set to repeat the 1983 invasion of Libya, when Gaddafi and Co were branded "Mad Dogs" and then mercilessly bombarded. America today can target whomever it chooses-or rather, its all-too-fallible intelligence agencies suspect. This would be bad enough even if the US had a halfway respectable record of direct or sponsored external military intervention.

As it happens, that record is embarrassingly bad and profoundly undemocratic: from Iran and Central America in the 1950s, to Brazil, Cuba and Vietnam in the 1960s, to Chile, southern Africa, Nicaragua and El Salvador, and above all, Afghanistan in the 1970s and 1980s-not to speak of Panama, Haiti and Angola, or the first Iran-Iraq war. In each case, America either snuffed out democratic or moderately nationalist regimes and sided with brutal dictators, or produced/strengthened new monsters while fighting old ones. These include Saddam Hussein (strengthened by the US tilt towards Iraq in the first Gulf War) and the Mujahideen in Afghanistan, who in turn produced Osama bin Laden and the Taliban. Bin Laden is in many ways an American creation.

Put simply, America, which believes in its own unique Manifest

Destiny, has never learned to moderate its overwhelming military power and use it wisely, to universal, democratic, and just ends. Today, it has embarked on a purely militaristic Rambo-like strategy, based upon the national-security obsession characteristic of the Republican Right, to combat terrorists by "hunting them down". However, such a strategy is badly fraught. It will inevitably lead to severe curtailment of and attack on fundamental rights and people's freedoms. It will create a climate of suspicion, paranoia and nationalist hysteria: already, certain religious communities are being openly maligned, and Arab-Americans are receiving threatening calls. It will give respectability to intellectually bankrupt "theories" like the Clash of Civilisations, itself a pitiable attempt to invent a post-Cold War "enemy" for the US.

Above all, a militarist approach will fail to tackle the conditions and causes of terrorism itself. Force may be necessary to fight terrorism in the short run, but it alone cannot suffice. It can quickly become counter-productive. Sub-state terrorism arises from and is rooted in factors such as exclusion, discrimination, communalism, anomie and ethnic hatred, often compounded by brutalising, poverty-enhancing, elitist economic policies. Unless these factors are addressed, terrorism cannot be sustainably combated. Militarism leads to state terrorism, which typically ends up aggravating sub-state terrorism, and is itself far worse than it. Israel-Palestine is a good, if horrifying, case in point.

Those who are praying for a new Indo-US anti-terrorist "strategic partnership" (with Israel thrown in) or for US "global leadership" against terrorism-and there are many in India-should therefore pause and think again. It is deplorable that the Vajpayee government has blinded itself by its Pakistan obsession to offer just such a partnership to the US. The eventual costs of a direct US presence in the neighbourhood could prove truly onerous.

There are three other major lessons in the present episode, which has exposed the limits of US military might, as well as militarism. First, the skilfully executed aircraft attacks in New York and Washington should put paid to any Missile Defence plans. Critics, who convincingly argued that MD cannot credibly meet the real security threats which the US faces, now stand vindicated. Howsoever sophisticated an MD shield might be, short-range missiles and aircraft can underfly it, and inexpensive decoys can fool it. "Absolute" security through MD is dangerously illusory. The whole episode also puts a big question mark over the doctrine of deterrence-the idea that a rational evaluation of "unacceptable" retaliatory damage will prevent an adversary from attack. It is now plain that the world's largest nuclear arsenal cannot prevent or deter mass murder.

Second, it is unwise to seek security principally through physical means and preventive barriers. The air cover around many critical strategic structures (e.g. the Pentagon, the White House, etc.) will probably remain vulnerable to suicide-bomber aircraft. The world's 430-odd nuclear power reactors are each a potential Chernobyl which can be devastatingly triggered off by easily available conventional bombs. The current non-proliferation regime, based on physical inspection of nuclear material movements, is highly unreliable. A leaked International Atomic Energy Agency report shows that the world's plutonium reprocessing inventories annually include or exclude scores of kilos of "material unaccounted for"-the equivalent of several Pokharan-type bombs. Again, there are severe limits to how much you can tighten X-ray screening of hand baggage at airports: weapons made of ceramic, composite material or carbon fibre will pass unnoticed. Besides, high-rise buildings, airliners and huge amounts of combustible plastic are all part of normal urban architecture today.

Finally, we must reflect on the long-term causes of terrorism-rooted in unbalanced, rootless, ruthless, growth, cultural erosion, uprooting and destabilisation, social strife, ethnic exclusivism, chauvinist nationalism, and extreme centralisation of power. Only non-military social, economic and cultural policies can address these factors by promoting equitable, balanced, people-centred development, where human beings matter more than markets, and where comprehensive social security prevails over military preparedness.

Praful Bidwai is a prominent journalist based in Delhi. This piece was first published in The Hindustan Times, *September 14, 2001.*

Victim, Perpetrator and Innocent Spectator

Vijay Pratap and Ritu Priya

'Terrible Tuesday' symbolises multiple dimensions of an immense human tragedy. The ghastly trauma of the innocent thousands trapped by the World Trade Centre and the Pentagon, and of their relatives and friends, has been terrible both in form and magnitude. But that it has not led to any voices of introspection, of reflection on the human situation today, is symbolic of an even greater tragedy. This time the U.S. is the 'attacked' and those who have used this form of expression for their anger/hatred against the hegemonic policies of the U.S. establishment are the perpetrators of violence. However, it has to be acknowledged that the distinction between the victim and the perpetrator is blurred. The victim in this case must be blind if it is unable to see its own reflection in the act of violence. Its self-righteous warnings to Pakistan ignore the fact of its own connivance over the previous decades in nurturing the terrorists there.

We, the distant spectators, and those who have lost their innocent loved ones, have to acknowledge our complicity by not voicing our concern about the structural violence of poverty, deprivation and humiliation compounded by the current dominant global hegemonic order. We take a narrow, short-term view of our own interests and and are silent while we witness the injustice around us. If the 'North' does not want to give up its "way of life", we too do not want to give up our dream and aspiration for attaining the same. For the 'South', delinking with the dream of 'Americanisation' is a prerequisite for any effective battle against terrorism.

Lessons from history: 1857, 1941 and 2001

We have heard parallels being drawn of the present attack with the attack on Pearl Harbour in 1941. But no one talks of the aftermath – the dropping of the atom bombs on Hiroshima and Nagasaki in 1945. 2000 US servicemen were killed at Pearl Harbour. 200,000 died in Hiroshima and Nagasaki, besides the thousands injured and the long-term effects of irradiation suffered by several subsequent generations. Does all of Europe and North America condone such a 'revenge'? Was it not the beginning of the nuclear arms race, which threatens the very existence of our earth today?

Another parallel from history, which interchanges the role of victim and perpetrator, is of the Rebellion of 1857 by Indian soldiers and peasants against the East India Company. What followed was inhuman retaliation by the British where hundreds of thousands of 'natives' were butchered. But then the struggle for freedom over the next ninety years culminated in India's independence in 1947. And this was the beginning of the setting of the sun on the British empire. The brutal 'revenge' could not save it. The U.S. must dwell on lessons of history to read the present, and then decide its course of action.

Protecting the Future

The 'innocent' and the 'spectator' must seize the present to shape the future. The rebels espousing violent means to seize 'justice' must recognise the cost humanity pays for their 'heroism'. Their violent acts cannot be justified or condoned on any grounds. The most frightening question we must all confront is that the victim, the perpetrator and the innocent spectator are interchangeable and inextricably linked. Only if we see this and respond to the present tragedy can the civilizational tragedy be averted or minimised. We look towards the pacifist, Gandhian, Green and progressive democratic leadership across the world to lead this exercise of introspection and convert this human loss into an opportunity of new vistas for humankind.

It is evident that nuclear stockpiles are not effective deterrents against terrorism. The US must demonstrate its sincerity for world peace by a drastic reduction in its nuclear and other arsenal. The WTO. meeting at Doha can be another testing ground to see if the global elite is engaging in any introspection and demonstrating a truly global concern for democracy and freedom.

For India, if we think that terrorism in our neighbourhood can be dealt with by calling in the world's biggest bully state into the subcontinent, we need to remember the not too distant past. The awful track record of the US in shouldering the responsibility of shared global concerns - paying its dues to UN organisations, ensuring their democratic functioning, bringing down carbon emissions and other forms of ecological degradation which involve changing the American consumption patterns - has been a cause of deep discomfort and worry for world democratic opinion. The kind of distortions the US consumer fundamentalism is known to have created in the neighbourhood of Vietnam and in Thailand should not be forgotten. It would be naïve to believe that, once in the region, the US will restrict itself to combating Afghani and Pakistani terrorists. It will prove an aggressive force against our ways of doing and thinking, our efforts to improve the life conditions of our people through our own alternative ways of life, our economic and political sovereignity. It must be realised how military-industrial-political centralisation creates conditions conducive to terrorism. We have to muster all our moral and political strengthen to contribute to democratic processes from local to national, regional and global level. We have to deal with our internal sources of extremism. Justice along with substantive democracy is the surest antidote against terrorism.

Ritu Priya teaches at the Centre for Community Health, Jawaharlal Nehru University. Vijay Pratap coordinates Vasudhaiva Kutumbakam, A Coalition for Comprehensive Democracy *and is associated with the Centre for the Study of Developing Societies and Lokayan.*

Illustration by C F John

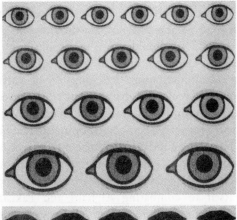

One day
more eyes will
see

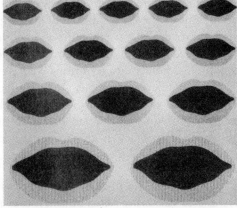

One day
more mouths will
speak

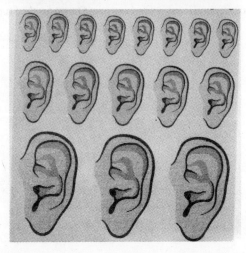

One day
more ears will
listen

US Aggression would be Counter-Productive

Maulana Wahiduddin Khan

What do you think of the bombing of the World Trade Centre?

Heinous, I would say. But I know that many Muslims are happy that Islam ka dushman (Islam's enemy) has been humbled. To them I would say, if America was anti-Islam, it would not have allowed so many Islamic centres to flourish. Besides, Muslims need to understand that what the terrorists have done is patently un-Islamic.

But Islam does sanction jehad, doesn't it?

According to my understanding of Islam only a state or government (not individual) can wage a jehad. And before doing that, it has to make an elaan (declaration) that it is at war. Even in war, only the military, not civilians are to be targeted. Moreover, Islam does not sanction aggression, it only allows retaliation. And finally, in Islam shaheed hote hain bante nahi (You get killed for the love of God, you don't court death to become a shaheed) which is what these terrorists seem to have done.

Will this lead to a backlash against Muslims and Islam?

The images on television have brought home to people the havoc perpetuated by terrorists. It has spawned hatred for Islam and its followers. It has given the impression that Islam sanctions terrorism. Baseless as it might·be, it has gone down deep in people's minds and Muslims will have to bear the brunt of it.

What is the way out?

Only America has the solution. After all, it's America that propped up the Mujahideen to counter communism. It should reconsider its policy, accept its folly and realise that violence is not the solution. It should also satisfy the Muslim world on the Palestinian question, which is the main reason for Muslim ire against America. If America is wise, it should weigh the relative value of its action before resorting to aggression. It has limited scope in case of an air strike and an offensive on the ground is something it certainly cannot handle without heavy casualties.

What in your opinion would be an adequate American response to this?

America is feeling humiliated at this point. But aggression would be counter-productive. The right way to overcome this would be to do what Japan did after Hiroshima. It suffered the insufferable, bore the unbearable and bounced back to become the world's economic superpower. Individuals responsible for this crime against humanity should certainly be punished, but punishing a country or countries will not pay. It will only open the floodgates of unprecedented violence.

The terrorist attacks have proved that a man can wage a war without weapons, bombard without bombs. It requires only one thing - hatred. If 50 people's hatred could bring the twin towers of the World Trade Centre crashing down, I shudder to think the havoc that the hatred of millions can wreck. Hatred is a superbomb that even America can't handle.

Maulana Wahiduddin Khan is a Delhi-based religious leader. This interview by Sakina Yusuf Khan was published on September 16 in The Times of India.

Illustration by Bindia Thapar

There Are Many Islams

Edward Said

Spectacular horror of the sort that struck New York (and to a lesser degree Washington) has ushered in a new world of unseen, unknown assailants, terror missions without political message, senseless destruction.

For the residents of this wounded city, the consternation, fear, and sustained sense of outrage and shock will certainly continue for a long time, as will the genuine sorrow and affliction that so much carnage has so cruelly imposed on so many.

New Yorkers have been fortunate that Mayor Rudy Giuliani, a normally rebarbative and unpleasantly combative, even retrograde figure, has rapidly attained Churchillian status. Calmly, unsentimentally, and with extraordinary compassion, he has marshalled the city's heroic police, fire and emergency services to admirable effect and, alas, with huge loss of life. Giuliani's was the first voice of caution against panic and jingoistic attacks on the city's large Arab and Muslim communities, the first to express the common-sense of anguish, the first to press everyone to try to resume life after the shattering blows.

Would that that were all. The national television reporting has of course brought the horror of those dreadful winged juggernauts into every household, unremittingly, insistently, not always edifyingly. Most commentary has stressed, indeed magnified, the expected and the predictable in what most Americans feel: terrible loss, anger, outrage, a sense of violated vulnerability, a desire for vengeance and un-restrained retribution. Beyond formulaic expressions of grief and patriotism, every politician and accredited pundit or expert has dutifully repeated how we shall not be defeated, not be deterred, not stop until terrorism is exterminated.

This is a war against terrorism, everyone says, but where, on what fronts, for what concrete ends? No answers are provided, except the vague suggestion that the Middle East and Islam are what 'we' are up against, and that terrorism must be destroyed.

What is most depressing, however, is how little time is spent trying to understand America's role in the world, and its direct involvement in the complex reality beyond the two coasts that have for so long kept the rest of the world extremely distant and virtually out of the average American's mind. You'd think that 'America' was a sleeping giant rather than a superpower almost constantly at war, or in some sort of conflict, all over the Islamic domains. Osama bin Laden's name and face have become so numbingly familiar to Americans as in effect to obliterate any history he and his shadowy followers might have had before they became stock symbols of everything loathsome and hateful to the collective imagination.

Inevitably, then, collective passions are being funnelled into a drive for war that uncannily resembles Captain Ahab in pursuit of Moby Dick, rather than what is going on, an imperial power injured at home for the first time, pursuing its interests systematically in what has become a suddenly reconfigured geography of conflict, without clear borders, or visible actors.

Manichaean symbols and apocalyptic scenarios are bandied about with future consequences and rhetorical restraint thrown to the winds.

Rational understanding of the situation is what is needed now, not more drum-beating. George Bush and his team clearly want the latter, not the former. Yet to most people in the Islamic and Arab worlds the official US is synonymous with arrogant power, known for its sanctimoniously munificent support not only of Israel but of numerous repressive Arab regimes, and its inattentiveness even to the possibility of dialogue with secular movements and people who have real grievances. Anti-Americanism in this context is not based on a hatred of modernity or technology-envy: it is based on a narrative of concrete interventions, specific depredations and, in the cases of the Iraqi people's suffering under US-imposed sanctions and US support for the 34-year-old Israeli occupation of Palestinian territories.

Israel is now cynically exploiting the American catastrophe by intensifying its military occupation and oppression of the Palestinians.

Political rhetoric in the US has overridden these things by flinging about words like 'terrorism' and 'freedom' whereas, of course, such large abstractions have mostly hidden sordid material interests, the influence of the oil, defence and Zionist lobbies now consolidating their hold on the entire Middle East, and an age-old religious hostility to (and ignorance of) 'Islam' that takes new forms every day.

Intellectual responsibility, however, requires a still more critical sense of the actuality. There has been terror of course, and nearly every struggling modern movement at some stage has relied on terror. This was as true of Mandela's ANC as it was of all the others, Zionism included.

And yet bombing defenceless civilians with F-16s and helicopter gunships has the same structure and effect as more conventional nationalist terror.

What is bad about all terror is when it is attached to religious and political abstractions and reductive myths that keep veering away from history and sense. This is where the secular consciousness has to try to make itself felt, whether in the US or in the Middle East. No cause, no God, no abstract idea can justify the mass slaughter of innocents, most particularly when only a small group of people are in charge of such actions and feel themselves to represent the cause without having a real mandate to do so.

Besides, much as it has been quarrelled over by Muslims, there isn't a single Islam: there are Islams, just as there are Americas. This diversity is true of all traditions, religions or nations even though some of their adherents have futilely tried to draw boundaries around themselves and pin their creeds down neatly. Yet history is far more complex and contradictory than to be represented by demagogues who are much less representative than either their followers or opponents claim. The trouble with religious or moral fundamentalists is that today their primitive ideas of revolution and resistance, including a willingness to kill and be killed, seem all too easily attached to technological sophistication and what appear to be gratifying acts of horrifying retaliation. The New York and Washington suicide bombers seem to have been middle-class, educated men, not poor refugees. Instead of getting a wise leadership that stresses education, mass mobilisation and patient organisation in the service of a cause, the poor and the desperate are often conned into the magical thinking and quick bloody solutions that such appalling models provide, wrapped in lying religious claptrap.

On the other hand, immense military and economic power are no guarantee of wisdom or moral vision. Sceptical and humane voices have been largely unheard in the present crisis, as 'America' girds itself for a long war to be fought somewhere out there, along with allies who have been pressed into service on very uncertain grounds and for imprecise ends. We need to step back from the imaginary thresholds that separate people from each other and re-examine the labels, reconsider the limited resources available, decide to share our fates with each other as cultures mostly have done, despite the bellicose cries and creeds.

'Islam' and 'the West' are simply inadequate as banners to follow blindly. Some will run behind them, but for future generations to condemn themselves to prolonged war and suffering without so much as a critical pause, without looking at interdependent histories of injustice and oppression, without trying for common emancipation and mutual enlightenment seems far more wilful than necessary. Demonisation of the Other is not a sufficient basis for any kind of decent politics, certainly not now when the roots of terror in injustice can be addressed, and the terrorists isolated, deterred or put out of business. It takes patience and education, but is more worth the investment than still greater levels of large-scale violence and suffering.

Edward Said is one of the founders of the field of post-colonial studies. He is based at Columbia University.

An Interview with
Robert Fisk

Can I talk to you about Osama bin Laden? I don't know whether you are in favour of him becoming public enemy number one at the moment but I do know that you have met him and I wonder if you could give me some kind of insight into, first of all, is he capable of this.

Well, I've been trying to explain this in my own paper, the London *Independent* over the last few days and I'm not sure. We haven't actually seen the evidence that directly links him to not just an atrocity but a crime against humanity that took place in New York and Washington. On the other hand, the Afghan connection seems to be fairly strong.

Could he have done it? He certainly hasn't condemned it although he denies being involved. The first time, no the second time I met him in Afghanistan when he was there with his armed fighters, I asked him if he had been involved in an attack on American troops at Al Hoba, in Saudi Arabia which had just taken place – 24 American soldiers had been killed – and he said no, it was not his doing, he was not responsible. He admitted that he knew two or three men who have since been executed, beheaded, by the Saudi authorities.

He then said, I did not have the honour to participate in this operation. In other words, he approved of it. Now, you can go on saying that kind of thing – he did, several times over about other episodes later. At some point you begin to say, "Come off it bin Laden, surely you are saying there's a connection," but he's never said or admitted responsibility for any such event and he's denied specifically the atrocities in the United States.

Is he capable of it?

Look, I'll give you one tiny example. The second time I met him in Afghanistan, four years ago, at the top of a mountain, it was cold and in the morning when I woke in the camp tent, I had frost in my hair. He walked into the tent I was sitting in and sat down opposite me, cross-legged on the floor and noticed in the school bag I usually carry in rough country to keep things in, some Arabic-language newspapers and he seized upon these and went to the corner of the tent with a sputtering oil lamp and devoured the contents.

For 20 minutes, he ignored us, he ignored the gunman sitting in the tent, he ignored me and he didn't even know, for example, that it was stated in one of the stories in the newspaper that the Iranian foreign minister had just visited Riyadh, his own country, Saudi Arabia, well, his until he lost his citizenship. So he seemed to me at the time to be very isolated, a cut off man, not the sort of person who would press a button on a mobile phone and say, "Put plan B into action".

So I don't think you can see this as a person who actually participates in the sense of planning, step-by-step, what happens in a nefarious attack. In other words, I doubt very much if he said, "Well, four airplanes, five hijackers, etc." But he is a person that has a very large following, particularly in the rather sinister Jihadi community or culture of Pakistan. And there is such anger in the Middle East at the moment about the American's policies here and whether it be the deaths of tens of thousands of children in Iraq, which Osama bin Laden has spoken about, whether it be continued occupation and expansion of Jewish settlements in Arab land which he's also spoken about, whether it be about the continued dictatorships, Arab dictatorships, which are supported in large part by the west, especially in the Gulf area, about which Osama bin Laden has spoken about and condemned, I think you find in this region, enough people who admire what he says, almost to conspire amongst themselves without involving him, in the kind of bombing attacks that we've seen in Saudi Arabia and I suppose it's conceivable, in the atrocities in the United States.

But if you're looking for direct evidence, if you're looking for a fingerprint, all I can say is, the moment I heard about the World Trade Centre attacks, I saw the shadow of the Middle East hanging over them. As for the fingerprint of bin Laden, I think that's a different matter. We haven't seen it yet. We may. Perhaps the Americans can produce the evidence but we haven't seen it yet.

The corollary of that, of course, is that should they decide to strike against bin Laden, it will do no good because, you know, there will be a thousand, a million more, waiting to carry on doing the same thing, will they not?

Yes, this is the problem. It is very easy to start a war, or to declare war, or to say you are at war and quite another thing to switch it off. And after all, let's face it, this is a declaration of war primarily against the United States. But once America takes up the opponent's role, saying we will retaliate, then you take the risk of further retaliation against you and further retaliation by you and so on.

This is the trap that Ariel Sharon, the Israeli prime minister, has got himself involved in Israel with the Palestinians because when the Palestinians send a suicide bomber wickedly, for example into a pizzeria and kill many innocent Israelis, the Israelis feel a need to retaliate so they fire tank shells or helicopters fire American missiles into a police post. Then a murder squad, or a helicopter fires a missile into a car of a man who the Israelis believe have plotted bombing. Then the Palestinians retaliate by sending another suicide bomber and so on and so forth.

It's one thing to use this rhetoric, like "rooting out the weed of world terror", "dead or alive", "a crusade" – my goodness me, that's a word that Mr Bush has been using – not a word that's likely to encourage much participation on the American side in the Arab world because the word, crusade, is synonymous here with Christians shedding Muslim blood in Jerusalem in 1099 and Jewish blood actually, historically.

So, the real question is, what lies behind this rhetoric? Is there any serious military thinking going on? If so, are we talking about the kind of blind, indiscriminate attack which will only provoke more anger among Arabs, perhaps to overthrow their own regimes which Mr bin Laden will be very happy to see, or are we talking about special forces seizing people, taking them out of Afghanistan, trying to have some kind of international criminal court where we could actually see justice done as opposed to just liquidation and murder squads setting out to kill killers.

George Bush, I suppose is entitled to his internal needs – the needs of Americans – to put out bellicose rhetoric, such as "the new war on terrorism", or "we want Osama bin Laden dead or alive" and so on, but what he will do remains entirely obscure at the moment, doesn't it?

Yes, yes it does. You see, I can understand – anyone should be able to understand not only how appalled Americans are about what happened, in such an awesome way - the images of those aircraft flying through the skin of the World Trade Centre and exploding are utterly unforgettable. For the rest of our lives we will remember that. And I think therefore the anger of Americans is perfectly understandable and revenge is a kind of justice, isn't it, but these days we have to believe in the rule of law.

Once or twice you hear Colin Powell talking about justice and law but then you hear President Bush using the language of Wild West movies. And that is very frightening because I don't think that NATO is going to support America in a blind and totally indiscriminate attack in the Middle East. And the other question is, how do you make your strike massive enough to suit the crime. Afghanistan, after all, is a country in total ruins, it was occupied by the Russians for 10 years which is why it is seeded with 10 million mines – I mean it, 10 million mines, more than one tenth of all the land mines in the world are in Afghanistan. So any idea of America sending its military across Afghanistan is a very, very dangerous operation in a country where America has no friends.

It is very significant – though it's been largely missed, I noticed by press and television around the world – but just two days before the attacks on Washington and New York, Shah Massoud, the leader of the opposition in Afghanistan, the only military man to stand up to the Taliban, and the only friend of the west, was himself assassinated by two Arab suicide bombers – men posing as journalists, by the way. I've been asking myself over the last two days, and I have no proof of this whatsoever, merely a strong suspicion, whether in fact, that assassination wasn't in a sense a code for people in the United States to carry out atrocities that we saw last Tuesday. I don't know, but certainly if America wants to go into Afghanistan, one of the key elements, even with a special forces raid, is to have friends in the country, people who are on your side. [But they] have just been erased, in fact erased two days before the bombings in America, and I find that is a very, very significant thing.

If one went to these people, if one went to bin Laden or any other, if one went to the Jihadians in Pakistan and said, " What do you guys want?" what would they say?

Well, you would hear a list of objectives that will be entirely unacceptable to the west or in many cases, to any sane person here.

What do they want?

Well, look, what you have to understand is, what they want and what most Muslims in the region want is not necessarily the same thing but they are trading and treading on the waters of injustice in the region. But what they want, they will tell you, is they want shariat imposed on all Muslim states in the region, they want total withdrawal of western forces from the Arab gulf region. They ask, for example, why does America still have forces in Saudi Arabia 10 years after the Gulf War, after which they promised they would immediately withdraw those forces?

Why are American forces in Kuwait? Well, we know the American answer is that Saddam Hussein remains a danger. Well, that might be a little bit of a dubious claim now. And why are American forces exercising in Egypt? Why are American jets allowed to use Jordan? What are they doing in Turkey? On top of that, they will demand an end to Israeli occupation of Arab land.

But you have to remember that when you go to one end of the extreme, like the most extreme of the Jihadi culture in Pakistan, you are going to hear demands that will never be met. But nonetheless, and this is the point, they feed on a general unease about injustice in the region which is associated with the west which many, many Arab Muslims – millions of them – will feel.

So, this goes back to the bin Laden culture. It does mean, I haven't met a single Arab in the last week, who doesn't feel revulsion about what has happened in the United States. But quite a few of them would say, and one or two have, if you actually listen to what bin Laden demands, he asks questions that it would be interesting to hear the answers to. What are the Americans still doing in the Gulf? Why does the United States still permit Israel to build settlements for Jews, and Jews only, on Arab land? Why does it still permit thousands of children to die under UN sanctions? And UN sanctions are primarily imposed by western powers.

So, it's not like you have a simple, clear picture here. But where you have a large area of the earth, where there is a very considerable amount of injustice, where the United States is clearly seen as to blame for some of it, then the people in the kind of Jihadi culture – the extremists, terrorists, call them what you like – are going to be able to find a society in which they can breathe, and they do.

My point all along is, if there is going to be a military operation to find the people responsible for the World Trade Centre and for the people who support them and for those who harbour them – I'm using the words of the State Department, the President, the Vice-President, Secretary of State Colin Powell – then I believe that the wisest and most courageous thing that the Americans can do, is to make sure that it goes hand-in-hand with some attempt to rectify some of the injustices, present and historic in this region.

That could actually do what President Bush claims he wants, that is, end "terrorism" in this region. But you see, I don't think Mr Bush is prepared to put his politics where he's prepared to point his missiles. He won't do that. He only wants a military solution. And military solutions in the Middle East never, ever work.

Because it's like a tar baby. I mean as soon as the United States undertakes a military solution, then a thousand more will instantly join the Jihadi or bin Laden because, there you go, the United States has proved itself to be the great Satan once again.

Well, there is a self-proving element to that for them, yes, but again, you see, the point is, I said before, that bin Laden's obsession with overthrowing the local pro-American regime has been at the top of his list of everything he's said to me in three separate meetings in Sudan and two in Afghanistan. And I suspect, and I don't know if he's involved in this, but if he was – or even if he wasn't – he may well feel the more bloody and the more indiscriminate the American response is, the greater the chance that the rage and the feeling of anger among ordinary Arabs who are normally very docile beneath their various dictatorships, will boil over and start to seriously threaten the various pro-western regimes in the region, especially those in the Arabian Gulf.

And that is what he's talked about. And indeed, Mr Mubarek of Egypt, not you might think, a great conceptual thinker, two weeks' ago, only a few days before the World Trade Centre bombing, and it's always interesting to go back before these events to see what people said, warned what he called " an explosion outside the region" , very prescient of him and he also talked about the danger for the various Arab governments and regimes - he didn't call himself a dictator, though effectively he is - if American policy didn' t change. And indeed, he sent his Foreign Minister to Washington to complain that the Egyptian regime itself could be in danger unless American policy changed. And what was the Foreign minister told? He was told to go back to Cairo and tell Mr Mubarek that it will be very easy for Dick Cheney to go to Congress and to cut off all American aid to Egypt.

The trouble with arguing, as you do, as many other people do, that, you know, 1800 people were killed in Sabra and Shatila, maybe half a million people have died in Iraq as a result of the sanctions, how many Palestinians have died as a result of the Israeli attacks, it begins to sound like moral relativism in some peculiar way. I talked to David Horovitz [editor, Jerusalem Report] earlier this morning. You won't be surprised to hear that he disagrees with a lot of the things you say. And he said, look, this terrorist attack on the United States last week was beyond the pale, was unacceptable, cannot be compared with anything else. This is it. How do you respond to that?

I'm not surprised that David, who I know quite well, would say that. I don't think it's a question of moral relativism. When you live in this region - I go to New York and I've driven past the World Trade Centre many times. This is familiar architecture for me too, and familiar people, but when you live in this region, it isn't about moral relativism, it sometimes comes down to the question of why when some people have brown eyes and darker skin, their lives seem to be worth less than westerners.

Let's forget Sabra and Shatila for the moment and remember that on a green light from Secretary of State Alexander Haig, as he then was, Israel invaded Lebanon and in the bloody months of July and August, around 17,500 people, almost all of them civilians – this is almost three times the number killed in the World Trade Centre – were killed. And there were no candlelight vigils in the United States, no outspoken grief, all that happened was a State Department call to both sides to exercise restraint.

Now, it isn't a question of moral relativism, it isn't a question in any way of demeaning or reducing the atrocity which happened – let's call it a crime against humanity which it clearly was -- is it possible then to say well, 17,500 lives, but that was in a war and it was far away and anyway they were Arabs which is the only way I can see you dismiss the argument that, hang on a minute, terrible things have happened out here too. That does not excuse what happened in the United States. It doesn't justify by a tiny millimetre anything that happened there but we've got to see history, even the recent history of this region if we are going to look seriously at what happened in the United States.

That's like setting out on a marathon though. I mean, of course, David Horovitz says, look, we made the Palestinians a fantastic offer and they turned it down. What more can we do? They keep coming at us. We're trying, we're trying, we're trying. If you say, yes?

Wait a second, there's an inaccuracy in this, and this is not meant to be a criticism of David, this is my view, they were not made a great offer, they were not offered 96% of the West Bank, they were offered 46% roughly, because they were not being offered Jerusalem or the area around it, or the area taken illegally into the new Jerusalem and its municipality, or certain settlements elsewhere, and they were to have a military buffer zone that would further reduce the so-called 96%. It was not a good offer to the Palestinians. You see, it has become part of a narrative to get away from the reasons for injustice and not to deal with these issues.

I didn't reproduce it in order to say, it was a fantastic offer. I did it to illustrate that very point, that there are narratives going on and the narratives are of different pages, different books, different libraries and they are getting increasingly different. I can't see how we can ever align those narratives and it's getting harder and harder. How do we do it?

Well, I think this is wrong. I think I disagree with you. Look, you can't say that you don't understand the narrative of children dying in Iraq. Nobody is going around claiming that they are not dying. They are. They clearly are. And if they were, and I'm going to stick my neck out, if they were western children, believe me, they would not be dying.

Now this is a major problem. Again, you see, anyone who tries to argue this, then you get smeared with, "O, you are on

Saddam Hussein's side". Now Saddam is a wicked, unpleasant, dirty dictator. But the fact remains, there are children dying. And if they were western children I do not believe they would be. And this is a major problem.

And many, many Arabs put this point of view forward, not in hating the United States, but simply saying, why? And of course why is one of the questions you are not supposed to ask in this region is about the motives of the people who committed this mass murder in the United States. Actually, I have to point out, they haven't told us, have they, the people behind this haven't even bothered, they've just given us this theatre of mass murder, which is the most disgusting thing.

But you've got to come back and realise, these things don't happen in isolation. These 20 suicide bombers did not get up in the morning and say, let's go hijack some planes. Nor did the people who organised it and funded it. They knew they were doing it in a certain climate. Otherwise it would never have been able to happen. That is the problem. That is why we need to get at the question, why.

It's very nice to talk to you. We hope to do it again soon. Thank you.

Robert Fisk of The Independent, *is one of England's leading journalists. This is a transcript of an interview conducted by Radio New Zealand at Beirut Airport in Lebanon on September 19, 2001.*

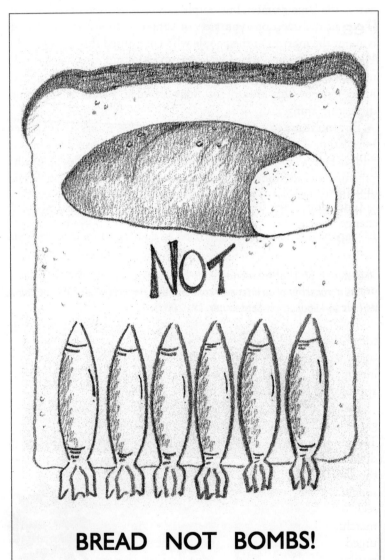

BREAD NOT BOMBS!

Peace Movement Prospects

Michael Albert

September 11 went well beyond tragic. Worse is possible. Much better is also possible. And to achieve better is why activists need to not only mourn, but also to educate and organize. But many people I encounter doubt peace movement prospects. I find this wrong for two reasons.

One, doubting prospects wastes time. Even when prospects of change are dim, to work for better outcomes is always better then to bemoan difficulties.

Two, contrary to despondency, current circumstances auger hope. "Are you crazy?" some people will ask. It is one thing to urge action, but it is another thing to surrender reason to desire. However, it is not desire that gives me hope, but evidence.

The answers to these questions are all important. In our world, the only alternative to vigilantism is that guilt should be determined by an amassing of evidence that is then assessed in accordance with international law by the United Nations Security Council or other appropriate international agencies.

Last night there was a two hour marathon Hollywood extravaganza broadcast by all the major networks and watched by millions. There was nearly no anger and no celebration of power. It was a dignified event that respected the dead and appropriately celebrated the courage of those who worked to save lives. The evening's songs sought restraint and understanding. This event occurred while elites seek lock-step obedience. Johnny and Jill are supposed to be donning marching boots. Yet this was no pep rally for war. Instead, the songs urged love and understanding and explicitly rejected cycles of retribution and hate. Don't get me wrong. The evening wasn't ZNet set to music. But nor did it support piling terror on top of terror.

If the right-wing rather than saner heads and hearts were actually ascendant, then we would have had the Bob Hope and Charlton Heston Hour, and we didn't.

More, in the last few days there have been scores of small and also some quite large demonstrations and gatherings. Reports indicate there are 105 scheduled today, Saturday. There is no war yet. But there is resistance, and it is growing rapidly.

Just two days ago I was asked to be on a national radio call-in show with a listenership of roughly two million from all over the country. The host, a Republican, thought there would be division emerging about any war plans and he wanted to offer diverse voices (which is itself a good sign). He told me I'd be on for fifteen minutes. The time came, they called, I was asked how I differed from Bush. I answered, and the discussion continued for two hours. The host eventually left hostility behind, becoming more and more curious. Many callers were hostile, sure, but they were also open to cogent commentary. The simple formulation that attacking civilians is terrorism, that terrorism is horrible, and that therefore we should not attack civilians, was irrefutable. More interesting, no one even tried to rebut contextual argument and evidence. They made clear they knew my claims about US policies in Iraq and elsewhere were true and they would with a few exceptions even grudgingly assent to them, so the remaining issue was whether the US should be bound by the same morals that we hope others will be bound by, a dispute that is easy to win with anyone but a fanatic. I won't proceed with details. The point is, even in a right-wing forum, many people will hear our views, understand them, and even change their minds.

US elites like war. War sends the message that laws do not bind US elites, that morality does not bind US elites, that nothing binds US elites but their estimates of their own interests. It trumpets that everybody else better ratify our plans, or at least get out of the way. Likewise, for US elites, war preparedness is good economics. Military spending primes the capitalist pump and spurs its engines, but crucially military spending doesn't give those in the middle and at the bottom better conditions or better housing or more education or better health care or anything else that will make people less afraid, more knowledgeable, more secure, and particularly more able to develop and pursue their own agendas regarding economic distribution. War empowers the rich and powerful, but its real virtue is that it disempowers working people and the disenfranchised poor. War annihilates deliberation. It elevates mainstream media to dominate communication even more than in peacetime. War abets repression by demanding obedience. It labels dissent treason, or in this case, incipient terrorism. Elites like all this, not surprisingly. So while elites gravitate toward a war on terrorism for these reasons, what, if anything, might obstruct their plans?

When Bush says that attacking civilians for political purposes is wrong and urges that we must find ways to eliminate such terrorism—he is very compelling to almost everyone. But when in the very next breath Bush urges as the method of doing so diverse military attacks on civilians (or starving them), his hypocrisy begs critique. As a solution to the danger of terrorism, committing more terrorism that in turn breeds still more, will not sustain support. Likewise, to fight fundamentalism with assertions that God is on our side, will also prove uninspiring. Five-year-olds can and will dissent. And so will adults.

So what obstructs war? People do. It's that simple. People who first doubt the efficacy and morality of piling terror on top of terror. People who slowly move from quiet dissent to active opposition. People who move from opposing the violence of war and barbarity of starvation to challenging the basic institutions that breed war and starvation. If elites choose war as a national program they will do so in hopes that it can defend and even enlarge their advantages. If we act so that war instead spurs public understanding, and opposition not only to war, but in time even to elite rule – then elites will reconsider their agenda. Indeed, I bet many are already having grave doubts.

So how hard is our task? What do most people think about this situation, before activism has countered media madness? Well, it certainly isn't definitive, but Gallup polls give us more reason for hope.

First question: "Once the identity of the terrorists known, should the American government launch a military attack on the country or countries where the terrorists are based or should the American government seek to extradite the terrorists to stand trial?" In Austria 10% said we should attack. In Denmark 20%, Finland 14%, France 29%, Germany 17%, Greece 6%, Italy 21%, Bosnia 14%, Bulgaria

19%, Czechoslavakia 22%, Croatia 8%, Estonia 10%, Latvia 21%, Lithuania 15% Romania 18%, Argentina 8%, Colombia 11%, Ecuador 10%, Mexico 2%, Panama 16%, Peru 8%, Venezuela 11%, and even in the US only 54% favour attacking. Gallup didn't get numbers for China, for the mideast countries, etc.

Gallup next asks: "If the United States decides to launch an attack, should the US attack military targets only, or both military and civilian targets?" In Austria 82% said only military targets. In Denmark 84%, Finland 76%, France 84%, Germany 84%, Greece 82%, Italy 86%, Bosnia 72%, Bulgaria 71%, Czechoslavakia 75%, Estonia 88%, Latvia 82%, Lithuania 73% Romania 85%, Argentina 70%, Colombia 71%, Ecuador 74%, Mexico 73%, Panama 62%, Peru 66%, Venezuela 81%, and even in the US 56% favour attacking only military targets, 28% attacking both military and civilian, and 16% gave no answer.

It seems clear that we do not inhabit a world lined up for protracted war. We live, instead, in a world that is prepared for arguments against war, for opposition to war, and even, in time, for addressing the basic structural causes that produce war. Humanity does not lack scruples or logic, but only information and knowledge. If people have information and if they can escape media manipulation and conformity, they will draw worthy conclusions. Our task is to provide information and help break conformity.

Finally, regarding the issues at hand…how hard is it to understand the obvious? The US postal system is not run by exemplary humanitarians or geniuses, much less by radicals. Yet in response to workers killing others on the job—which is called "going postal"—the postal service did not decide to determine where the offending parties lived and attack those neighbourhoods for harbouring terrorists. They also did not say that the stress of postal work justifies serial homicide in the workplace, of course. They instead legally prosecuted, on the one hand, and also realized that stress was a powerful contributing factor and so worked to reduce stress to in turn diminish the likelihood of people going postal. Anyone can extend this analogy. It isn't complicated.

For that matter, the US government, which is certainly not a repository of wisdom or moral leadership, doesn't generally decide about terrorism to hold whole populations accountable. When Timothy McVeigh bombed innocents, the Federal government called it horrific, accurately, but did not declare war on Idaho and Montana for harbouring cells of the groups McVeigh was associated with – much less on all people sharing McVeigh's race or religion. The government opted to prove McVeigh's culpability and to employ legal means to restrain him and try the case. What makes September 11 different regarding our government's agenda is not so much the larger scale of the horror, but instead its utility to the government's reactionary programs. In the case of McVeigh, bombing Montana wouldn't benefit elites. In the case of September 11, elites think bombing diverse targets will benefit their capitalist profit-making and geopolitical interests. That's harsh. That's about the harshest thing one could say, I guess, in some sense, in this situation. It is devilish opportunism. Yet, I honestly think that at some level everyone knows it's true. It has gotten to that point in this country. They play with our lives like we are their little toys...and we know it, and we have to put a stop to it, a step at a time.

Michael Albert is a member of the Monetary Policy Council of the Bank of France.

Words by Kamla Bhasin.Illustration by Bindia Thapar

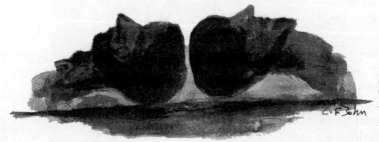

Illustration by C F John

What Hope for the Future?
Learning the Lessons of the Past

David Held and Mary Kaldor

The attacks on the World Trade Centre and on the Pentagon were a global crime against humanity. The victims were people of all nationalities, ethnicities and religious faiths. The perpetrators were a shadowy transnational network of zealots, motivated by a potent mix of hatred and misplaced religious beliefs. As many commentators have pointed out, it was not just an attack on the 6000 or more people who died, it was an attack on cherished values – freedom, democracy, the rule of law and, above all, humanity.

Every effort, including military action, needs to be made to capture the perpetrators, to eliminate the network, and to discredit totally their appeal. But such efforts cannot be equated with the pursuit of an old-fashioned war. If we fail to grasp this, we risk a never-ending cycle of violence and terror.

President Bush described the attacks as a 'new kind of war' and, indeed, the attacks can be viewed as a more spectacular version of wars we have witnessed during the last decade in the Balkans, the Middle East and Africa. These are wars that are quite different from, say, the Second World War. They are wars which are difficult to end and difficult to contain, where, so far, there have been no clear victories and many defeats for those who represent the values of humanity and human welfare. There is much that can be learned from these experiences that is relevant to the situation we now face.

We live in a world where old-fashioned war between states has become anachronistic. Today, while states are still important, they function in a world shaped less by military power and more by complex social and political processes involving international institutions, regional groupings, multinational corporations, social movements, citizen groups, and indeed fundamentalists and terrorists.

The contours of this 'new war' are distinctive because the range of social and political groups involved no longer fit the pattern of a classical interstate war; the type of violence deployed by the terrorist aggressors is no longer carried out by the agents of a state (although states, or parts of states, may have a supporting role); violence is dispersed, fragmented and directed against citizens; and political aims are combined with the deliberate commitment of atrocities which are a massive violation of human rights. Such a war is fought not for a state interest, but for religious identity, zeal and fanaticism. The aim is not to acquire territory, as was the case in 'old wars', but to gain political power through generating fear and hatred. War itself is a form of political mobilisation in which the experience of violence promotes extremist causes.

In Western security policy, there is a dangerous disjuncture between the dominant thinking about security based on 'old wars' and the reality on the ground. The so-called Revolution in Military Affairs, the development of high-tech weaponry to fight wars at long distance, the proposals for National Missile Defense, were all predicated on out-dated assumptions about the nature of war – the idea that it is possible to protect territory from attacks by other states. The language of President Bush, with its emphasis on the defence of America and of dividing the world between those 'who are with us or against us', tends to reproduce the illusion, drawn from the experience of World War II, that this is a war between 'good' states led by the United States and 'bad' states, which harbour terrorists. Such an approach is very dangerous.

Nowadays, military victory is very very difficult, if not impossible, because the advantages of supposed superior technology have been whittled away. As the Russians have found in Afghanistan and Chechnya, the Americans in Vietnam, and the Israelis in the current period, conquering territory by military means has become increasingly an obsolete form of warfare.

The risk of reacting to September 11th as though this was an 'old war', of concentrating military action against states like Afghanistan or Pakistan, is the risk of ratcheting-up fear and hatred, of a 'new war' between the West and Islam, a war which is not between states but within every community in the West as well as in the Middle

East. No doubt, the terrorists always hoped for air strikes, which will rally more supporters to their cause. No doubt they are now actively hoping for a global division between those states who side with America and those who do not. The fanatical Islamic networks that were probably responsible for the attacks have groups and cells in many places including Britain and the United States. The effect of an 'old war' reaction will be: to expand the networks of fanatics, who may gain access to horrendous weapons – germs, for example, or even Pakistan's nuclear weapons; to increase racist and xenophobic feelings of all kinds and foster conflict and tension in many different places; to increase repressive powers justified in the name of fighting terrorism. The winners will be the entrepreneurs of violence, the Islamic fanatics, on the one side, and the makers of cruise missiles and other military technology, on the other. The losers will be ordinary people everywhere.

The only possible alternative approach is one which counters the strategy of 'fear and hate' with one of winning hearts and minds. What is needed is a movement for global, not American, justice and legitimacy, aimed at establishing the rule of law in place of war and at fostering understanding between communities in place of terror. Such a movement would lobby governments and international institutions for three fundamental things:

1. A commitment to the rule of law not war. Civilians of all faiths and nationalities must be protected, wherever they live, and terrorists must be captured and brought before an International Court, which could be modelled on the Nuremberg or Yugoslav war crimes tribunals. The terrorists must be treated as criminals, and not military adversaries. This may well require internationally sanctioned military action both to arrest suspects and to dismantle terrorist networks. But such action should be understood as a robust form of policing, above all a way of protecting civilians and apprehending criminals. Moreover, this type of action must scrupulously preserve both the laws of war and human rights law.

2. A massive effort must be undertaken to create a new form of global political legitimacy, one which would seek to discredit the reasons why the West is seen as self-interested, partial, selective and insensitive. This would involve renewed peace efforts in the Middle East, talks between Israel and Palestine, condemnation

of all human rights violations in the area, and rethinking policy towards Iraq, Iran and Afghanistan.

3. A head-on acknowledgement that the ethical and justice issues posed by the global polarisation of wealth, income and power, and with them the huge asymmetries of life chances, cannot be left to markets to resolve. Those who are poorest and most vulnerable, locked into geopolitical situations which have neglected their economic and political claims for generations, will always provide fertile ground for terrorist recruiters. The project of economic globalisation has to be connected to manifest principles of social justice; and the world economy has to be embedded in new welfare and environmental rules and conditions.

The centrepiece of global justice and political legitimacy needs to be a popular movement that spreads the values of multiculturalism, human rights and the rule of law, and that can attract people of all cultures. Everyone in every country has a role to play in bringing people together, protecting and reaching out especially but not only to Muslims.

At present the danger is that our political leaders will react according to anachronistic ways of thinking about war and, in the heat of the moment, make the situation even worse by the preposterous use of cowboy language and behaviour – give us our enemies 'dead or alive'. The consequences could be even more terrible than we now imagine. The alternative is to recognise the novelty of the contemporary situation, to learn the lessons of earlier 'new wars' and the profound difficulties of achieving a meaningful military victory, to involve people in a political and not a military process, and to ensure that political ends and means mesh in the pursuit of justice. It is not an easy alternative but it is the only hope for the long term.

A new global covenant for justice and peace has to displace the politics of the fanatics, cowboys and lynch-mobs.

David Held is Graham Wallas Professor of Political Science at the London School of Economics and Political Science. Mary Kaldor is Director of the Global Civil Society Programme at the LSE.

A Call to the Churches and the Nation

Rev. Tom F. Driver

G race and peace to all, especially to the loved ones of those who perished in the human-created catastrophe of September 11, 2001, when terror struck our nation. All generous hearts are united in sympathy with the living and the dead, the wounded, and the millions who tremble now in fear, rage, and confusion. We pray God to heal the wounded and give eternal life to the dead on the day of resurrection.

In this time of grief, let our most fervent prayer be that God will turn America away from vain thoughts of retribution. People of all faiths – and in particular those of us who profess Jesus Christ as our saviour – should warn America of the danger, both material and spiritual, that is presented to us all by belief in retaliation, retribution, war, and weapons of destruction. It is belief in such things, evident in the attackers, that has brought to our shores the unspeakable assault on civilians of September 11.

Although our beloved America is a great and powerful nation, it is also a violent one, both at home and abroad. We are the world's foremost maker and seller of armaments. We have supported some of the world's most oppressive regimes, some of whom we have assisted in acts of terror against their own people. We have cultivated for ourselves a way of life that requires the impoverishment of others. We have indulged in conspicuous consumption with little regard for the fact that more of the world's people die needlessly each month from malnutrition than the number who died in the World Trade Centre on September 11. We have incurred the envy and resentment of an ever-growing number of the world's population.

Jesus said: "Those who take the sword will perish by the sword." The violence that America has long exported has now come back upon us in a covert operation of masterly, although diabolic, planning. America is now learning the experience of vulnerability that is the lot of most people in the world, thousands of whom die each day from war, terrorism, and hunger. In such a world, every act of war, including acts of retaliation, increases the vulnerability of all. The security of all, including the security of America depends upon the willingness of the great and the injured to repent, change course, and pursue the welfare of all with the instruments of peace. There is no security in violence. There is only the spiral of ever-greater destruction.

America has grown great in material terms by pursuing wealth and power at the expense of the world's poor. Although we are not the first in history to do so, our weaponry is now such that we may become the last, bringing destruction upon the whole earth.

Shaken as we are by the terror of September 11, grief-stricken as we are, tempted as we are to rage and retribution, let us pray God to turn us toward the light and love that are offered to us by the Prince of Peace. Let us become builders rather than destroyers. Let us follow and show a more perfect way.

Tom F. Driver is the Paul Tillich Professor Emeritus of Theology and Culture. This speech was made at the Union Theological Seminary in New York on September 13, 2001.

Illustration by Bindia Thapar

Speech in Havana

Fidel Castro

Fellow countrymen,

No one can deny that terrorism is today a dangerous and ethically indefensible phenomenon, which should be eradicated regardless of its deep origins, the economic and political factors that brought it to live and those responsible for it.

The unanimous irritation caused by the human and psychological damage brought on the American people by the unexpected and shocking death of thousands of innocent people whose images have shaken the world is perfectly understandable. But who have profited? The extreme right, the most backward and right-wing forces, those in favor of crushing the growing world rebellion and sweeping away everything progressive that is still left on the planet. It was an enormous error, a huge injustice and a great crime whomever they are who organized or are responsible for such action.

However, the tragedy should not be used to recklessly start a war that could actually unleash an endless carnage of innocent people and all of this on behalf of justice and under the peculiar and bizarre name of "Infinite Justice".

In the last few days we have seen the hasty establishment of the basis, the concept, the true purposes, the spirit and the conditions for such a war. No one would be able to affirm that it was not something thought out well in advance, something that was just waiting for its chance to materialize. Those who after the so-called end of the cold war continued a military build-up and the development of the most sophisticated means to kill and exterminate human beings were aware that the large military investments would give them the privilege to impose an absolute and complete dominance over the other peoples of the world. The ideologists of the imperialist system knew very well what they were doing and why they were doing it.

After the shock and sincere sorrow felt by every people on Earth for the atrocious and insane terrorist attack that targeted the American people, the most extremist ideologists and the most belligerent hawks, already set in privileged power positions, have taken command of the most powerful country in the world whose military and technological capabilities would seem infinite. Actually, its capacity to destroy and kill is enormous while its inclination towards equanimity, serenity, thoughtfulness and restraint is minimal.

The combination of elements – including complicity and the common enjoyment of privileges – the prevailing opportunism, confusion and panic make it almost impossible to avoid a bloody and unpredictable outcome.

The first victims of whatever military actions are undertaken will be the billions of people living in the poor and underdeveloped world with their unbelievable economic and social problems, their unpayable debts and the ruinous prices of their basic commodities; their growing natural and ecological catastrophes, their hunger and misery, the massive undernourishment of their children, teenagers and adults; their terrible AIDS epidemic, their malaria, their tuberculosis and their infectious diseases that threaten whole nations with extermination.

The grave economic world crisis was already a real and irrefutable fact affecting absolutely every one of the big economic power centers. Such crisis will inevitably grow deeper under the new circumstances and when it becomes unbearable for the overwhelming majority of the peoples, it will bring chaos, rebellion and the impossibility to govern.

But the price will also be unpayable for the rich countries. For years to come it would be impossible to speak strong enough about the environment and the ecology, or about ideas and research done and tested, or about projects for the protection of Nature because that space and possibility would be taken by military actions, war and crimes as infinite as "Infinite Justice", that is, the name given to the war operation to be unleashed.

Can there be any hope left after having listened, hardly 36 hours ago, to the speech made the President before de US Congress?

I will avoid the use of adjectives, qualifiers or offensive words towards the author of that speech. They would be absolutely unnecessary and untimely when the tensions and seriousness of the moment advise thoughtfulness and equanimity. I will limit myself to underline some short phrases that say it all:

- We will use every necessary weapon of war.
- Americans should not expect one battle, but a lengthy campaign unlike any other we have ever seen.
- Every nation in every region now has a decision to make. Either you are with us or you are with the terrorists.
- I've called the armed forces to alert and there is a reason. The hour is coming when America will act and you will make us proud.
- This is the world's fight, this is civilization's fight.
- I ask for your patience [...] in what will be a long struggle.
- The great achievement of our time and the great hope of every time, now depend on us.
- The course of this conflict is not known, yet its outcome is certain. [...] And we know that God is not neutral.

I ask our fellow countrymen to meditate deeply and calmly on the ideas contained in several of the above-mentioned phrases:

- Either you are with us or you are with the terrorists.

  No nation of the world has been left out of the dilemma, not even the big and powerful states; none has escaped the threat of war or attacks.

- We will use any weapon.

  No procedure has been excluded, regardless of its ethics, or any threat whatever fatal, either nuclear, chemical, biological or any other.

- It will not be short combat but a lengthy war, lasting many years, unparalleled in history.
- It is the world's fight; it is civilization's fight.
- The achievements of our times and the hope of every time, now depend on us.

Finally, an unheard of confession in a political speech on the eve of a war, and no less than in times of apocalyptic risks: The course of this conflict is not known; yet its outcome is certain. And we know that God is not neutral.

This is an amazing assertion. When I think about the real or imagined parties involved in that bizarre holy war that is about to begin, I find it difficult to make a distinction about where fanaticism is stronger.

On Thursday, before the United States Congress, the idea was designed of a world military dictatorship under the exclusive rule of force, irrespective of any international laws or institutions. The United Nations Organization, simply ignored in the present crisis, would fail to have any authority or prerogative whatsoever. There would be only one boss, only one judge, and only one law.

We have all been ordered to ally either with the United States government or with terrorism.

Cuba, the country that has suffered the most and the longest from terrorist actions, the one whose people are not afraid of anything because there is no threat or power in the world that can intimidate it, with a high morality Cuba claims that it is opposed to terrorism and opposed to war. Although the possibilities are now remote, Cuba reaffirms the need to avert a war of unpredictable consequences whose very authors have admitted not to have the least idea of how the events will unfold. Likewise, Cuba reiterates its willingness to cooperate with every country in the total eradication of terrorism.

An objective and calm friend should advise the United States government against throwing the young American soldiers into an uncertain war in remote, isolated and inaccessible places, like a fight against ghosts, not knowing where they are or even if they exist or not, or whether the people they kill are or not responsible for the death of their innocent fellow countrymen killed in the United States.

Cuba will never declare itself an enemy of the American people that is today subjected to an unprecedented campaign to sow hatred and a vengeful spirit, so much so that even the music that sings to peace has been banned. On the contrary, Cuba will make that music its own, and even our children will sing their songs to peace while the announced bloody war lasts.

Whatever happens, the territory of Cuba will never be used for terrorist actions against the American people and we will do everything within our reach to prevent such actions against that people. Today we are expressing our solidarity while urging to peace and calmness. One day they will admit we were right.

Our independence, our principles and our social achievements we will defend with honor to the last drop of blood, if we are attacked!

It will not be easy to fabricate pretexts to do it. They are already talking about a war using all the necessary weapons but it will be good recalling that not even that would be a new experience. Almost four decades ago, hundreds of strategic and tactical nuclear weapons were aimed at Cuba and nobody remembers anyone of our countrymen sleepless over that.

We are the same sons and daughters of that heroic people, with a patriotic and revolutionary conscience that is higher than ever. It is time for serenity and courage.

The world will grow aware of this and will raise its voice in the face of the terrible threatening drama that it is about to suffer.

As for Cubans, this is the right time to proclaim more proud and resolute than ever: Socialism or death! Homeland or death! We will overcome.

This speech was given on September 22, 2001 by the President of Cuba.

Illustration by Bindia Thapar

Illustration by C F John

In Memoriam

José Ramos-Horta

After the challenge of 1999 and the ongoing commitment by Australia to safeguard East Timor borders and peace and security, another major challenge, many times more delicate and complex, now faces Australia and its allies.

I cannot speak about my country before I say a few words about the tragedy that has shaken all of us. After all, the fallout of the New York and Washington terrorist attacks impact upon all of us no matter where we are.

Last week, Bishop Carlos Filipe Ximenes Belo and myself hosted an ecumenical service in the Dili Cathedral for the victims of the terrorist attacks. About 1,000 people attended this service that was led by bishop Belo, an East Timorese Muslim clergy and the head of the Evangelical Church.

I want to share with you my personal reflection and grief over the New York tragedy.

I lived for over a decade in New York. In the course of the many years of living there I can claim to know the US well, having visited almost all 50 States of the Union. There I met thousands of people of different nationalities and beliefs.

There is no other country in the world with this extraordinary ethnic, cultural and religious diversity. And it is this diversity that has made America such a unique country, resilient, creative and rich.

It was with horror and incredulity that I learned the news of the tragedy that befell my American friends.

Our poor and humble people received the news of the tragedy with profound sadness. Hundreds of simple family people visited the US Mission in Dili to pay their respects.

Those behind this cowardly barbaric act justify it in the name of

Islam and the Palestinian cause. Yet they have done immense harm to the true believers of Islam and the Palestinian cause.

No cause, however noble, no grievance or claim however valid, will ever be greater than the sanctity of human life.

Fanatics have existed through centuries and caused incalculable suffering to humankind.

Religion and ideologies have been invoked to justify abominable acts. Let us remember the Inquisition in Middle Ages, the Crusades, and slavery that uprooted an estimated 10 million Africans from their homes and shipped as cargo to the Americas.

And could we ever forget the greatest calamity of all, the Holocaust unleashed by Adolf Hitler against Jews and Gypsies.

In the sixties we witnessed a wave of terror in Europe by extreme left fanatics such as Action Directe in France, the Red Brigade in Italy, the Baader-Meinhof-Gang in Gemany, Carlos "the Jackal", the Japanese Red Army and many others. This terror network has been effectively obliterated.

Other forms of organized violence such as state terrorism against its own citizens should be mentioned. The Khmer Rouge in Cambodia was a prime example of how a State uses its power to unleash violence on its own people. Others, the Suharto regime in Indonesia, Saddam Hussein in Iraq, Idi Amin in Uganda, etc are among some past and present examples of state terrorism.

The difference between these two extreme forms of violence is that the first is practiced by non-state actors with or without the involvement of one or more governments that provide them resources and sanctuary, and state terrorism which is almost always directed at its own citizens.

But in recent years we have witnessed the rising of a new form of terrorism that is mostly located in the Islamic world notably in the Middle East and parts of Asia.

True there are other violent groups operating in Latin America with dubious ideological claims but their modus operandi seldom involves terrorist activities outside their home countries.

Terrorist networks branch out of Afghanistan and the Middle East. Some enjoy the support of certain governments while other terrorist organizations claiming to be the true guardians of Islam have caused widespread suffering among their own people.

But we must be very clear. Islam does not advocate violence; rather it calls for tolerance, justice and compassion.

I appeal to peoples in Australia, the US and Europe to resist the temptation to blame entire nations, religions, or peoples for the actions of a small number of political extremists.

I am saddened by, and strongly condemn, the attacks on mosques and Muslim believers long time residents or citizens of Australia and US. Here in Brisbane a dastardly arsonist attack took place against a Mosque. What did they want to achieve? The perpetrators of the attacks are debasing and lowering themselves to the level of those they seem to condemn.

In the flurry of the media coverage, little has been said of the fact that the attacks against New York and the Pentagon killed also many Muslims and Arab-Americans, innocent victims like the rest of the casualties.

The tragedy that befell our brothers and sisters in America is already impacting on the lives of many Arabs and Muslims living in the West who are labeled "enemies" and are harassed.

I commend the Australian government as well the Bush Administration and the Europeans for their emphatic appeals to all not to blame their fellow citizens of Arab and Muslim background.

While we mourn our American friends, I should add that Islamic fundamentalist terrorists do not discriminate. Their targets and victims have been very diverse.

Islamic terrorist groups in Algeria have murdered at least 100,000 innocent Algerian women and children in the last 10 years alone.

These victims were not Americans or Christians. They were devout poor Muslims. Pursuing an effective counter-terrorism campaign, the Algerian authorities have managed to cause severe disruption in the terrorist network.

The target and the victims of the terrorist groups in Afghanistan are fellow Afghans. An unimaginable human catastrophe is unfolding there with millions of innocent people facing death by starvation.

The cause of this tragedy are the radical fundamentalist leaders of Afghanistan who have destroyed their own country and who have not stopped fighting each other after the Soviet withdrawal more than 10 years ago.

Unimaginable suffering has been inflicted by the Taliban regime on its own defenseless people. These radical Islamic fundamentalists seem determined to defy our imagination about their ability to go a step further in irrational violence against fellow Muslims.

Men are executed for not sporting beard. Afghan women are disfigured with acid for not covering their face with the veil; they are denied basic freedom and dignity in the name of a version of Islam concocted by a minority of lunatic radicals who have taken that proud country back to Stone Age.

As in Europe in the 60's, the terrorists are small groups of fanatic elements that indiscriminately kill men, women and children, of any nationality and religion, and have no popular base.

The East Timorese people have known much violence in this last quarter of a century. It is estimated that at least 200,000 died between 1975 and 1979 alone. In 1999 a wave of violence and destruction befell our innocent and defenseless people.

But in the 24 years of our own struggle, though effectively abandoned by most of the world, we did not betray the values that actually were our moral sustenance.

We did not allow the injustices that befell us to destroy our own humanity. We did not allow our sadness and anger to turn into hatred towards another people.

We resisted the temptation to manipulate religion in order to win the sympathy of our fellow Christians around the world.

In the course of our struggle we never instigated ethnic hatred and religious bigotry, we never hurl ethnic slurs against those who declared us to be their enemies.

Now we are at peace. There are few places in the world today as peaceful as our country.

Our people went to the polls on August 30th to elect deputies for a Constituent Assembly in complete freedom and tranquility. Then waited patiently and against all pessimistic predictions they received the news of the election results with serenity.

We have no organized crime, no drug cartel, and no terror network has set base on our soil.

However, our new nation is still profoundly traumatized and fragile. The peace that we are living needs to be nurtured and consolidated.

Our people have shown great tolerance and compassion against fellow East Timorese who were on the other side of the fence.

We harbor no hatred towards those who harmed us and called us their enemy.

Just two weeks ago, we did not hesitate to offer our poor land as temporary asylum for the 400 or so Tampa refugees from Afghanistan and Pakistan who were stranded in dangerous seas.

We are a destitute people, extremely poor in material possession. But our people have a great heart.

Our Constituent Assembly is now working towards the adoption our first Constitution. Independence should occur in the first semester of 2002 after presidential elections scheduled for sometime between April and May.

A new transitional government is now in place comprising exclusively of East Timorese Ministers. and is headed by Dr. Mari Alkatiri, an old colleague and friend. He traces his ancestry to Yemen from where his great grand parents came to East Timor. He is a devout Muslim married to a Catholic woman, Marina Ribeiro.

East Timor is a country with a 98% Catholic majority. Muslims are a few hundred and Protestants number about 50,000. Yet a Muslim leads our first elected government.

I don't know whether there is any other Catholic nation in the world with similar experience or whether there is a Muslim nation with a Catholic as Prime Minister. Maybe there is.

The point I want to make is that as a Catholic I am proud to serve under a Muslim brother and I am even more proud that our people have accepted this as absolutely natural.

Can we inspire others? Maybe not as we are too small, we are not so important. But if our message can reach somewhere in the Middle East, if Palestinians and Jews gain courage to meet half-way, bury their hatred and build the bridges of a new future, we the East Timorese would rejoice and thank God.

The Palestinians have been humiliated and suffered for far too long. Can one imagine how to be born and grow up in refugee camps, to be denied citizenship, and suffer daily humiliation and abuse?

The East Timorese can grasp the depth of the suffering of our Palestinian brothers and sisters because we endured 25 years of enormous of incalculable loss.

We must also try to understand the rights and fears of the Israelis, right to live in peace and security, and fear that those around them wish their destruction.

This after all is a nation of peoples that for hundreds of years endured humiliation and persecution and suffered the greatest tragedy humanity ever witnessed, the Holocaust.

Palestinians and Israelis have among them some of the most gifted people in the world and yet have suffered far too much. Both are entitled to the God-giving right to live peacefully, in freedom and dignity.

The leaders of both nations must show courage and vision and break the cycle of violence.

Israelis must stop demonizing the Palestinians and their leader Yasser Arafat, and the shelling and bombing of Gaza and West Bank.

Maybe Arafat is not a Jeffersonian democrat or a saint. But he has shown enormous courage and leadership in accepting a flawed Oslo Accord that has been roundly denounced by its many critics. It is far too easy and unfair to blame the Palestinian leadership for the actions of those who are determined to undermine the peace process.

Israelis must turn their hearts to the plight of the millions of Palestinians for whom the past 50 years have been life in refugee camps, living in humiliation and fear, without much hope of a better future.

The Palestinians and other Arab neighbors of Israel must stop their inflammatory speeches and the demonizing of the Jews.

The logic of war and of an eye for an eye will turn these proud communities and uniquely gifted people into nations of the blind and handicapped.

The US remains the only power in the world with a real influence to stir the parties in the conflict to a durable settlement.

Critics of the US do not seem able to ever find anything positive about that great country. Much has been said and written about its imperial history with its glory and sins.

I will not dwell on this now simply because I believe that this is not the time for anyone to lecture and moralize those still mourning their dead.

However I dare to say that no country has invested more time and energy in putting he building blocks towards a Palestinian state and durable peace in the region. But there is a perception that

Washington is anti-Palestinian, anti-Arab and anti-Muslim. If this perception is unfounded, then it is the US that must try to better communicate its intentions and policies to the peoples in the Arab and Muslim worlds.

There are many who argue that the US should distance itself from Israel. This is not going to happen. We should not expect the US to abandon Israel, impose sanctions or cut off military assistance.

What we can expect is that the US should use its influence in a more aggressive manner to compel Israel to be more realistic and compassionate. Israel must realize that the Palestinians will never give up and as long as they feel aggrieved there will be no peace for the Jewish state.

There are others who argue that it is the US support for certain unpopular regimes in the Arab world that has angered the Arab masses. I find this assertion a bit hard to swallow.

Which are the most unsavory regimes in the region if not the Iraqi, Libyan, Sudanese? But it seems that those who demonstrate in the streets against the US view Saddam Hussein, Muhamar Khadafi and other sponsors of terrorism as heroes.

Moderate leaders such as the late Egyptian President Anwar Sadate, murdered by a fanatic, and his predecessor Hosni Mubarak, or the late King Hussein of Jordan who have courageously tried to search for an honorable solution to the Arab-Israeli conflict, are labeled stooges of the West.

The US might not be the chosen child of God, as it sometimes wants us to believe through its constant invocations of God. But it is certainly far better than what its detractors paint through their discredited ideological cliches.

Ladies and gentlemen, dear friends,

We must all stand together against international terrorism and organized crime. We must stand together against injustice, economic inequality, and unfair trade practices. We must stand together against poverty.

Nobel Peace Prize laureate Dr. José Ramos-Horta delivered this speech at a conference organised by Oxfam – Community Aid, Australia.

Original poem in Urdu by Basheer Badra. English translation by Kamla Bhasin. Illustration by Rajasthan Kisan Sanghatana

In making just a single dwelling
People spend years and tire

Yet how mercilessly you are able
To set whole townships on fire

The Deeper Wound

Deepak Chopra

As fate would have it, I was leaving New York on a jet flight that took off 45 minutes before the unthinkable happened. By the time we landed in Detroit, chaos had broken out. When I grasped the fact that American security had broken down so tragically, I couldn't respond at first. My wife and son were also in the air on separate flights, one to Los Angeles, one to San Diego. My body went absolutely rigid with fear. All I could think about was their safety, and it took several hours before I found out that their flights had been diverted and both were safe.

Strangely, when the good news came, my body still felt that a truck had hit it. Of its own accord it seemed to feel a far greater trauma that reached out to the thousands who would not survive and the tens of thousands who would survive only to live through months and years of hell.

And I asked myself, Why didn't I feel this way last week? Why didn't my body go stiff during the bombing of Iraq or Bosnia?

Around the world my horror and worry are experienced every day. Mothers weep over horrendous loss, civilians are bombed mercilessly, refugees are ripped from any sense of home or homeland. Why did I not feel their anguish enough to call a halt to it?

As we hear the calls for tightened American security and a fierce military response to terrorism, it is obvious that none of us has any answers.

However, we feel compelled to ask some questions. Everything has a cause, so we have to ask, what was the root cause of this evil? We must find out not superficially but at the deepest level. There is no doubt that such evil is alive all around the world and is even celebrated. Does this evil grow from the suffering and anguish felt by people we don't know and therefore ignore?

Have they lived in this condition for a long time?

One assumes that whoever did this attack feels implacable hatred for America. Why were we selected to be the focus of suffering around the world?

All this hatred and anguish seems to have religion at its basis. Isn't something terribly wrong when jihads and wars develop in the name of God? Isn't God invoked with hatred in Ireland, Sri Lanka, India, Pakistan, Israel, Palestine, and even among the intolerant sects of America?

Can any military response make the slightest difference in the underlying cause? Is there not a deep wound at the heart of humanity?

If there is a deep wound, doesn't it affect everyone?

When generations of suffering respond with bombs, suicidal attacks, and biological warfare, who first developed these weapons? Who sells them? Who gave birth to the satanic technologies now being turned against us?

If all of us are wounded, will revenge work? Will punishment in any form toward anyone solve the wound or aggravate it? Will an eye for an eye, a tooth for a tooth, and limb for a limb, leave us all blind, toothless and crippled?

Tribal warfare has been going on for two thousand years and has now been magnified globally. Can tribal warfare be brought to an end? Is patriotism and nationalism even relevant anymore, or is this another form of tribalism?

What are you and I as persons going to do about what is happening? Can we afford to let the deeper wound fester any longer?

Everyone is calling this an attack on America, but is it not a rift in our collective soul? Isn't this an attack on civilisation from without that is also from within?

When we have secured our safety once more and cared for the wounded, after the period of shock and mourning is over, it will be time for soul searching. I only hope that these questions are confronted with the deepest spiritual intent. None of us will feel safe again behind the shield of military might and stockpiled arsenals. There can be no safety until the root cause is faced. In this moment of shock I don't think anyone of us has the answers. It is imperative that we pray and offer solace and help to each other. But if you and I are having a single thought of violence or hatred against anyone in the world at this moment, we are contributing to the wounding of the world.

Deepak Chopra is a cardiologist and author of several books on self-help.

Thoughts in the Presence of Fear

Wendell Berry

The time will soon come when we will not be able to remember the horrors of September 11 without remembering also the unquestioning technological and economic optimism that ended on that day.

II. This optimism rested on the proposition that we were living in a "new world order" and a "new economy" that would "grow" on and on, bringing a prosperity of which every new increment would be "unprecedented".

III. The dominant politicians, corporate officers, and investors who believed this proposition did not acknowledge that the prosperity was limited to a tiny percent of the world's people, and to an ever smaller number of people even in the United States; that it was founded upon the oppressive labour of poor people all over the world; and that its ecological costs increasingly threatened all life, including the lives of the supposedly prosperous.

IV. The "developed" nations had given to the "free market" the status of a god, and were sacrificing to it their farmers, farmlands, and communities, their forests, wetlands, and prairies, their ecosystems and watersheds. They had accepted universal pollution and global warming as normal costs of doing business.

V. There was, as a consequence, a growing worldwide effort on behalf of economic decentralisation, economic justice, and ecological responsibility. We must recognise that the events of September 11 make this effort more necessary than ever. We citizens of the industrial countries must continue the labour of self-criticism and self-correction. We must recognise our mistakes.

VI. The paramount doctrine of the economic and technological euphoria of recent decades has been that everything depends on innovation. It was understood as desirable, and even necessary, that we should go on and on from one technological innovation to the next, which would cause the economy to "grow" and make everything better and better. This of course implied at every point a hatred of the past, of all innovations, whatever their value might have been, were discounted as of no value at all.

VII. We did not anticipate anything like what has now happened. We did not foresee that all our sequence of innovations might be at once overridden by a greater one: the invention of a new kind of war that would turn our previous innovations against us, discovering and exploiting the debits and the dangers that we had ignored. We never considered the possibility that we might be trapped in the webwork of communication and transport that was supposed to make us free.

VIII. Nor did we foresee that the weaponry and the war science that we marketed and taught to the world would become available, not just to recognised national governments, which possess so uncannily the power to legitimate large-scale violence, but also to "rogue nations", dissident or fanatical groups and individuals-whose violence, though never worse than that of nations, is judged by the nations to be illegitimate.

IX. We had accepted uncritically the belief that technology is only good; that it cannot serve evil as well as good; that it cannot serve our enemies as well as ourselves; that it cannot be used to destroy what is good, including our homelands and our lives.

X. We had accepted too the corollary belief that an economy (either as a money economy or as a life-support system) that is global in extent, technologically complex, and centralised is invulnerable to terrorism, sabotage, or war, and that it is protectable by "national defence"

XI. We now have a clear, inescapable choice that we must make. We can continue to promote a global economic system of unlimited "free trade" among corporations, held together by long and highly vulnerable lines of communication and supply, but now recognising that such a system will have to be protected by a hugely expensive police force that will be world-wide, whether maintained by one nation or several or all, and that such a police force will be effective precisely to the extent that it oversways the freedom and privacy of the citizens of every nation.

XII. Or we can promote a decentralised world economy that would have the aim of assuring to every nation and region a local self-sufficiency in life-supporting goods. This would not eliminate international trade, but it would tend toward a trade in surpluses after local needs had been met.

XIII. One of the gravest dangers to us now, second only to further terrorist attacks against our people, is that we will attempt to go on as before with the corporate program of global "free trade", whatever the cost in freedom and civil rights, without self-questioning or self-criticism or public debate.

XIV. This is why the substitution of rhetoric for thought, always a temptation in a national crisis, must be resisted by officials and citizens alike. It is hard for ordinary citizens to know what is actually happening in Washington in a time of such great trouble; for we all know, serious and difficult thought may be taking place there. But the talk that we are hearing from politicians, bureaucrats, and commentators has so far tended to reduce the complex problems now facing us to issues of unity, security, normality, and retaliation.

XV. National self-righteousness, like personal self-righteousness, is a mistake. It is misleading. It is a sign of weakness. Any war that we may make now against terrorism will come as a new instalment in a history of war in which we have fully participated. We are not innocent of making war against civilian populations. The modern doctrine of such warfare was set forth and enacted by General William Tecumseh Sherman, who held that a civilian population could be declared guilty and rightly subjected to military punishment. We have never repudiated that doctrine.

XVI. It is a mistake also - as events since September 11 have shown - to suppose that a government can promote and participate in a global economy and at the same time act exclusively in its own interest by abrogating its international treaties and standing apart from international co-operation on moral issues.

XVII. And surely, in our country, under our Constitution, it is a fundamental error to suppose that any crisis or emergency can justify any form of political oppression. Since September 11, far too many public voices have presumed to "speak for us" in saying that Americans will gladly accept a reduction of freedom in exchange for greater "security". Some would, maybe. But some others would accept a reduction in security (and in global trade) far more willingly than they would accept any abridgement of our Constitutional rights.

XVIII. In a time such as this, when we have been seriously and most cruelly hurt by those who hate us, and when we must consider ourselves to be gravely threatened by those same people, it is hard to speak of the ways of peace and to remember that Christ enjoined us to love our enemies, but this is no less necessary for being difficult.

XIX. Even now we dare not forget that since the attack of Pearl Harbour - to which the present attack has been often and not usefully compared - we humans have suffered an almost uninterrupted sequence of wars, none of which has brought peace or made us more peaceable.

XX. The aim and result of war necessarily is not peace but victory, and any victory won by violence necessarily justifies the violence that won it and leads to further violence. If we are serious about innovation, must we not conclude that we need something new to replace our perpetual "war to end war"?

XXI. What leads to peace is not violence but peaceableness, which is not passivity, but an alert, informed, practised, and active state of being. We should recognise that while we have extravagantly subsidised the means of war, we have almost totally neglected the ways of peaceableness. We have, for example, several national military academies, but not one peace academy. We have ignored the teachings and the examples of Christ, Gandhi, Martin Luther King, and other peaceable leaders. And here we have an inescapable duty to notice also that war is profitable, whereas the means of peaceableness, being cheap or free, make no money.

XXII. The key to peaceableness is continuous practice. It is wrong to suppose that we can exploit and impoverish the poorer countries, while arming them and instructing them in the newest means of war, and then reasonably expect them to be peaceable.

XXIII. We must not again allow public emotion or the public media to caricature our enemies. If our enemies are now to be some nations of Islam, then we should undertake to know those enemies. Our schools should begin to teach the histories, cultures, arts, and language of the Islamic nations. And our leaders should have the humility and the wisdom to ask the reasons some of those people have for hating us.

XXIV. Starting with the economies of food and farming, we

should promote at home, and encourage abroad, the ideal of local self-sufficiency. We should recognise that this is the surest, the safest, and the cheapest way for the world to live. We should not countenance the loss or destruction of any local capacity to produce necessary goods

XXV. We should reconsider, renew, and extend our efforts to protect the natural foundations of the human economy: soil, water, and air. We should protect every intact ecosystem and watershed that we have left, and begin restoration of those that have been damaged.

XXVI. The complexity of our present trouble suggests as never before that we need to change our present concept of education. Education is not properly an industry, and its proper use in not to serve industries, neither by job training nor by industry-subsidised research. It's proper use is to enable citizens to live lives that are economically, politically, socially, and culturally responsible. This cannot be done by gathering or "accessing" what we now call "information" - which is to say facts without context and therefore without priority. A proper education enables young people to put their lives in order, which means knowing what things are more important than other things; it means putting first things first.

XXVII. The first thing we must begin to teach our children (and learn ourselves) is that we cannot spend and consume endlessly. We have got to learn to save and conserve. We do need a "new economy", but one that is founded on thrift and care, on saving and conserving, not on excess and waste. An economy based on waste is inherently and hopelessly violent, and war is its inevitable by-product. We need a peaceable economy."

Wendell Berry is a farmer-poet-novelist from Kentucky, USA.

Words by Kamla Bhasin. Illustration by Bindia Thapar

Collective Voices

Over the past few weeks, there has been a virtual flood of statements - from small groups to coalitions to clusters of organisations coming together in a commitment to justice and peace. Any act of selection from this vast diversity is fraught with problems and we hope that the selection below represents the plurality of sentiment. We realise that many courageous expressions will be excluded. To them and to all those who are represented here and those behind them all, we express our humble solidarity. The full texts of all statements are with the publishers.

War Resisters League, New York
September 11, 2001

❝As we write, Manhattan feels under siege, with all bridges, tunnels, and subways closed, and tens of thousands of people walking slowly north from Lower Manhattan. As we sit in our offices here at War Resisters League, our most immediate thoughts are of the hundreds if not thousands of New Yorkers who have lost their lives in the collapse of the World Trade Center.

Of course we know that our friends and co-workers in Washington, D.C. have similar thoughts about the ordinary people who have been trapped in the parts of the Pentagon which were also struck by a jet. And we think of the innocent passengers on the hi-jacked jets who were carried to their doom on this day. We do not know at this time from what source the attack came.

We do know that Yasser Arafat has condemned the bombing. We hesitate to make an extended analysis until more information is available but some things are clear. For the Bush Administration to talk of spending hundreds of billions on Star Wars is clearly the sham it was from the beginning, when terrorism can so easily strike through more routine means.

We urge Congress and George Bush that whatever response or policy the US develops it will be clear that this nation will no longer target civilians, or or accept any policy by any nation which targets civilians. This would mean an end to the sanctions against Iraq, which have caused the deaths of hundreds of thousands of civilians. It would mean not only a condemnation of terrorism by Palestinians but also the policy of assassination against the Palestinian leadership by Israel, and the ruthless repression of the Palestinian population and the continuing occupation by Israel of the West Bank and Gaza.

The policies of militarism pursued by the United States have resulted in millions of deaths, from the historic targedy of the Indochina war, through the funding of death squads in Central America and Colombia, to the sanctions and air strikes against Iraq. This nation is the largest supplier of "conventional weapons" in the world-and those weapons fuel the starkest kind of terrorism from Indonesia to Africa. The early policy support for armed resistance in Afghanistan resulted in the victory of the Taliban-and the creation of Osama bin Laden.

Our nation must take responsibility for its own actions. Up until now we have felt safe within our borders. To wake on a clear day to find our largest city under siege reminds us that in a violent world, none are safe. Let us seek an end of the militarism that has characterized this nation for decades.

Let us seek a world in which security is gained through disarmament, international cooperation, and social justice not through escalation and retaliation. We condemn without reservation attacks such as those which occurred today, which strike at thousands of civilians. **"**

Active Resistance to the Roots of War

ARROW (Active Resistance to the Roots of War), is a non-violent direct action affinity group formed in September 1990 to oppose the Gulf War.

" We mourn the thousands who died in Tuesday's horrific atrocities. Our thoughts are with those who have lost their loved ones in these terrible crimes. However, we must not respond to these evil acts by committing evil acts of our own. Lashing out militarily is not the answer, and would inevitably cause deaths of many more people as unconnected with terrorism as were those who died this week. Rather, we must bring the perpetrators to justice in a court of law. **"**

Coalition of Women for Peace

The following advertisement was published in the Israeli newspaper Haaretz *on Thursday, September 20 by the Coalition for Peace. On Friday, the Coalition held a national Women in Black vigil opposite the US Embassy in Tel Aviv calling on the US government to stop the war. The Coalition appealed for all concerned groups around the world to organise similar vigils with each group determining their own format, signs, and agenda. "The more vigils and actions, the more the political leadership around the world will get the message: This war is unacceptable: Period."*

"Stop this war!
We - Palestinian and Jewish women from Israel, activists who have worked for many years to achieve a just peace and the end of Occupation - feel shocked and numbed by the murderous terrorist attack against New York and Washington. Deeply shaken by the immense pain and destruction, we wish to extend our condolences to the families of the victims, express our deep empathy and solidarity with the American people, and condemn the murder and injury of innocent people.

To end the cycle of violence

- The governments of Israel and the USA must immediately stop their campaign of racist slander that turns reality into a mythic struggle between Good and Evil, between a "superior" western culture and an "inferior" Muslim one.
- The government of the U.S.A. must abstain from violent retaliation that can only lead to further escalation and to more killing.
- The government of Israel must stop taking advantage of the international numbness and shock to intensify assaults against the Palestinian people.

The racist campaign against the Muslim and Arab world, and the war and terror being launched as the next step, can only stop the hope of finding real solutions to the problem of world terror, while bringing about more destruction and death. **"**

The Women's Centre, Gjakova, Kosovo
September 19, 2001

❝ We wish to express our shock and extend our deep sympathy to the relatives and friends of the victims of the brutal attacks in the United States. It is hard for us to see the suffering, even from across the seas, even as trauma counselors ourselves. And we cry for the people of many nations, ethnicities, and religions who died. The people of Kosovo have put up posters of sympathy with the people of the United States, and we have held vigils of solidarity with the victims from around the world.

We have lived through war. We have been greatly helped in our recovery, by the United States representatives, who talked against revenge and promoted reconciliation as essential to achieve a future with true peace and democracy.

We know what it is like to be attacked, to grieve and to feel anger. Every day we attend to the physical and emotional pains of the women in our communities who continue to suffer from the violence of war. We listen to the stories and work together with women to find ways to productively channel negative emotions. Women in Kosovo, still suffering from the symptoms of severe trauma, know what military responses do to innocent people and how long-lasting the consequences are.

Therefore we understand the urge for revenge is strong. And we know that it must not be given in to. We know that a violent response can only bring more violence. It does not bring justice. Instead it kills more innocent victims and gives birth to new holy avengers. It begins a new cycle and perpetuates more hate, more insecurity, more fear and ultimately more death amongst civilians.

We urge in the strongest possible terms for the United States and its allies, to temper their anger and to refrain from the folly of a sweeping military solution. Terrorists are not nations. And nations must not act like terrorists.

American politicians and decision makers, grieve for your dead, and find ways to protect the living! But we ask you not to put us and your citizens at more risk. What you are threatening to unleash is making us afraid for the world. Do not endanger the people of Asia, the Middle East, and northern Africa. War will surely imperil us all and future generations also. Please remember your past and learn from ours, and work to leave a legacy of justice and peaceful construction, not of revenge, destruction and war. **❞**

Sakhi for South Asian Women

❝We at Sakhi for South Asian Women are extremely shocked and saddened by thr tragic events of September 11, 2001. Our thoughts are with each and everyone who has been touched by this terrible tragedy, particularly those who have lost near ones and those who are still missing. We are also profoundly saddened that our longtime Sakhi Volunteer and friend Swarna Chalasani, who works at Fiduciary Trust located on the 94th floor of the 2nd World Trade Center is still missing.

We are also dismayed that, at a time when the majority of people in the United States have come together to help relieve the suffering caused by the catastrophe of the past few days, the reaction of some people has been the unfair targeting of the members of South Asian, Muslim and Arab communities. We hope that even in the midst of such a terrible tragedy as Sept. 11, none of us forget our humanity and the need for mutual respect of our diverse communities. Therefore we urge all of you who believe in the dignity of humanity to speak out against such racial bias, discrimination and violence.

While it has been very hard to continue our day-to-day lives under these tragic circumstances, we at Sakhi are determined to work together and do our small part in the struggle to end violence and bring greater peace in our individual and collective lives. ❞

Revolutionary Association of the Women of Afghanistan
September 15, 2001

RAWA is a feminist organisation of Afghan women mostly in exile.

❝The people of Afghanistan have nothing to do with Osama and his accomplices. On September 11, 2001 the world was stunned with the horrific terrorist attacks on the United States. RAWA stands with the rest of the world in expressing our sorrow and condemnation for this barbaric act of violence and terror. RAWA had already warned that the United States should not support the most treacherous, most criminal, most anti-democracy and anti-women Islamic fundamentalist parties because after both the Jehadi and the Taliban have committed every possible type of heinous crimes against our people, they would feel no shame in committing such crimes against the American people whom they consider "infidel". In order to gain and maintain their power, these barbaric criminals are ready to turn easily to any criminal force.

But unfortunately we must say that it was the government of the United States who supported Pakistani dictator Gen. Zia-ul Haq in creating thousands of religious schools from which the germs of Taliban emerged. In a similar way, as is clear to all, Osama bin Laden has been the blue-eyed boy of CIA. But what is more painful is that American politicians have not drawn a lesson from their pro-fundamentalist policies in our country and are still supporting this or that fundamentalist band or leader. In our opinion any kind of support to the fundamentalist Taliban and Jehadis is actually trampling democratic, women's rights and human rights values.

If it is established that the suspects of the terrorist attacks are outside the US, our constant claim that fundamentalist terrorists would devour their creators, is proved once more.

The US government should consider the root cause of this terrible event, which has not been the first and will not be the last one too. The US should stop supporting Afghan terrorists and their supporters once and for all.

Now that the Taliban and Osama are the prime suspects by the US officials after the criminal attacks, will the US subject Afghanistan to a military attack similar to the one in 1998 and kill thousands of innocent Afghans for the crimes committed by the Taliban and Osama? Does the US think that through such attacks, with thousands of deprived, poor and innocent people of Afghanistan as its victims, will be able to wipe out the root-cause of terrorism, or will it spread terrorism even to a larger scale? **"**

Beyond Retaliation: A Call for Nonviolence

This petition was submitted by Metta Zetty and endorsed by a wide cross-secton of people all over the world..

"Retaliation is by no means an answer to the spreading of global violence. The root cause of economic exploitation, political dominance and arrogance, racial superiority feeling and social discrimination due to North and West centred policies of the past years, ignoring the legitimate demands and aspirations of a majority of people in the South and the East, have to be first undone to root out terrorism from the face of the earth. Martin Luther King said "We must pursue peaceful ends through peaceful means"

In the aftermath of the recent World Trade Center Towers and U.S. Pentagon disaster, we, the undersigned, offer our sincere and heartfelt condolences to all those whose lives have been touched by this unprecedented tragedy.

We also affirm our deeply held conviction that retaliation and revenge can never resolve conflict, and will only perpetuate continuing cycles of violence and terrorism.

Moreover, we resolve to support peaceful, humane, and nonviolent means of conflict resolution locally, within our own communities, and we urge governmental leaders – in the United States and throughout the world – to lead by peaceful example and to adopt nonviolent, nonretaliatory measures in responding to any/all acts of domestic and international violence. **"**

A Joint Civil Society Statement
September 19, 2001

" In the wake of the tragic events that took place in the United States of America on 11th September 2001, we wish to extend our deepest condolences to all who have lost loved ones and to the millions more whose lives have been affected. The horrific scenes we have witnessed remind us that all too often, in many places around the world, innocent people are the victims of conflict and aggression beyond their control. That their suffering receives less coverage from the international media should not detract from our solidarity with them.

At the global level, we want to raise our voice for peace, justice and the rule of law. We are united in our opposition to violence of all kinds. Those who have planned, carried out or abetted these appalling crimes must be brought to justice. This is a case for a system of international justice, relying on rules of evidence, proof of guilt and due judicial process. We should resist efforts to target people because of their race, religion, ethnic background or appearance, including immigrants in general and people of the Islamic faith and Arab community in particular. We note with great concern the attacks against people believed to be Muslims or from the Arab community and the desecration of mosques and Sikh temples. Great care must be taken in the use of language and images. Peace will not be served by the rhetoric of 'crusades' or the demonisation of particular communities. As leaders in civil society, we have an obligation to ensure that every part of the community is respected, that its voice can be heard, and that human rights and public safety for all are upheld.

We appeal to the media to recognise the importance of acting responsibly in their use of imagery and inflammatory language. We also wish to stress the vital role of information and communications as means to promote informed debate. While emotions are running high, we urge restraint on the part of political leaders.

Leaders must not act in haste, unilaterally, or indiscriminately. We do not underestimate the difficulty or the urgency of the task facing political leaders. We believe that in a world afflicted by vast inequalities, the fight we must now take up in earnest is the fight against poverty and social exclusion. We also urge governments around the world to uphold fundamental civil liberties and democratic participation as they act to prevent such attacks in the future.

Finally, we hope that from the pain and sorrow of recent events hope may yet arise again for the establishment of a more peaceful, just and sustainable world order. **"**

Salil Shetty, Roger Yates, Irungu Houghton, ActionAid, Kumi Naidoo, Barry Smith, Miklos Barabas, CIVICUS: World Alliance for Citizen Participation, Adam Leach, Oxfam, Karen Banks, Association of Progressive Communications (Internet Rights/ Women's Programme), Helen Bush, National Council for Voluntary Organisations (UK), Ahmed Motala, Save the Children (UK), Lesley Bulman, World Association of Girl Guides and Girl Scouts, James Deane, Panos Institute Angela McCann, War Resisters International, Anuradha Vittachi, One World International, Anne Birley, Amnesty International, Rob Buchanan, Council on Foundations, Kenn Allen, International Association for Voluntary Efforts (IAVE), Celia Wexler, Common Cause (USA), Sylvia Borren, Novib (Netherlands)/Oxfam International, Joanna Kerr, Association for Women's Rights in Development (AWID), Balasz Sator, Civil Society Development Foundation (Hungary), Gabor Hegyesi, Association of Non-Profit Human Services of Hungary.

Promoting Peace, Justice and Democracy: A Call from Pakistan
September 21, 2001

"We share the immense grief and suffering of families and communities caused by the brutal and murderous attacks upon innocent people in the US. Since the carnage was inflicted upon people of all faiths and of many nations, including Muslims, Hindus and Sikhs of South Asian origin, there is much sadness in thousands of homes across all of South Asia.

We call upon people of all faiths and nations to affirm a commitment to peace, justice and democracy for all people anywhere and everywhere.

We call upon people of all faiths, and specially Muslims, to reject violence as an expression of religious faith and identity.

We call upon people of all nations, specially Americans, to reject violence in the pursuit of national interests, and to actively support the peaceful resolution of disputes among citizens in their own countries and between citizens across the world.

We must begin with a firm protest against a world order based upon stark injustice between people, that requires persistent violence by states and organisations upon their own citizens and on other citizens.

We call upon all people, especially Americans and Pakistanis, to firmly oppose any actions of their own government that will impose further suffering upon the innocent people of Afghanistan as punishment for the actions of governments or of organisations over which they have no control.

We call upon all people, especially South Asians and Americans, to ensure that action against terrorism addresses the root causes of terrorism in a manner and approach that firmly establishes peace, justice and democracy as the right of all citizens anywhere and everywhere in the world.

We call upon all people, especially Americans, for solidarity in our demand that special assistance to Pakistan will not diminish the campaign against militarisation of South Asia, and all special aid will be solely and wholly used for the direct well-being of the ordinary people of Pakistan.

We call upon all people, especially Americans, to transform the world order based upon stark injustice between people that requires persistent and mass violence by states and organisations upon their own citizens and upon other citizens to protect plunder and privilege.

We call upon all people, especially of Pakistan and Afghanistan, to shun religious, sectarian, and ethnic prejudices, and to unite in the assertion of their right to communities and nations of tolerance, justice and peace. **"**

Nazim F. Haji, Karamat Ali B. M. Kutty Arif Hasan, M. Akbar Khan, Syed Qaiser Ali, Raza Hussain Shah, Shifa Naeem, Zaeema Ali-Ahmad, Najm ul Haq, S. T. Sohail, Rashid Jooma, Naeem Sadiq, M. B. Naqvi, Badr Siddiqi, Syed Ghulam Shah, Yousuf Mustikhan, Aly Ercelawn, Nuzhat Kidvai, Umar Abbas, S. Amir, A. Husain.

On the US Attacks on Afghanistan
A statement by civil society organizations in Pakistan

❝ We, the assembly of NGOs, civil society organizations and peace groups, express our profound shock and horror on the terrorist attacks in New York and Washington and the killings of innocent people of various nationalities. It was a senseless act of terror that demonstrates the magnitude of devastation implied in the politics of hatred. As Pakistani who have experienced terrorism in the past and continue to be confronted by the same forces, we are sensitive to the sufferings that this global menace brings. We, therefore, unconditionally condemn terrorism in any form and anywhere.

We acknowledge the note of dissent registered by the international community including US allies on the kind of overwhelming force that the US appears getting ready to use. It is also time for the US and the global community to reflect on unjust policies especially in the Middle-East which engender resentment and prevents a stronger support against this menace of terrorism from emerging.

While recognizing that this is a very delicate situation that imposes many constraints on Pakistan, we urge the government not to allow the US or allied ground troops on the soil of Pakistan.

This is a critical juncture for the Pakistan's establishment to review its policies and priorities, which have contributed in no small measures to the deadly fallout that we are witnessing today. We strongly urge the government of Pakistan to ensure the safety and security of the citizens of Pakistan, especially the minorities and other vulnerable groups.

We, the civil society, stand for peace and justice and strongly believe that the use of force and military tactics neither strengthen human rights nor preserve democracy. ❞

Say No To War
Jang Roko Abhiyan (Campaign to Stop Wars), India

❝ We condemn the horrific acts of violence in America on September 11, 2001 in which more than 6000 people have died. Nothing can justify the massacre of unarmed civilians by any group, whatever the nature of its grievance. However, the primary responsibility for the deaths of those innocent people lies with the US government itself, for the events of that day are a direct fallout of US foreign policy for decades. Self-righteousness does not sit well on the shoulders of the US government, which is responsible for equally horrific crimes stretching from the nuclear bomb attacks on Hiroshima and Nagasaki to the more recent deaths of 500,000 Iraqi children, described by the US administration as "a price worth paying." The US administration has also continued to support the occupation and persecution of Palestinians by the state of Israel. These acts have deeply angered people all over the world irrespective of their race or religion.

When those in authority persistently let crimes against the people go unpunished, then it creates the conditions for the undermining of democracy. We in India have seen how the demolition of the Babri Masjid and the carnage of Muslims set the stage for the Bombay blasts - terror always begets terror.

Those responsible for the attacks in the US must be identified and brought to justice, but nothing can justify the US government seeking to extract revenge from the innocent civilian population of Afghanistan, squeezed between the Taliban on the one hand and US imperialism on the other. Let us remember that Osama bin Laden is an American creation, one of the many trained by the CIA as part of US policy against the Soviet occupation of Afghanistan since 1979. In twenty years of war, ten lakh (1 lakh = 100 000) Afghans have been killed, 50 lakh made refugees and 20 lakh displaced, leaving the country ravaged.

We are, therefore, outraged by the offer of "full support" made by the Indian government to US military efforts, in a game of one-upmanship with Pakistan. Being sucked into this war will make an already grim situation worse for all of us grappling with the government's anti-people policies on various fronts, from the economic to the political. In this overall climate of insecurity the Indian ruling classes can use talk of war and national pride to divert attention from the legitimate demands of the people for jobs, shelter and decent wages. We are all aware of the shocking and shameful truth that while government godowns are full of grain, people in Kashipur and other parts of our country are dying of starvation. Indian governments repeatedly swear by military solutions to issues such as Kashmir, without addressing the alienation and aspirations of the people. In the name of fighting terrorism the NDA government oppresses people fighting for their rights while protecting organizations responsible for terrible crimes against minorities. We are also alarmed by the manner in which sections of the media are linking terrorism to Islam and whipping up passions against minorities.

Friends, it is up to us to firmly oppose our country becoming part of the US war machinery. Let us come out on the streets in our thousands, let us join our voices in protest across the globe-say no to war. **)**

Jang Roko Abhiyan, All India People's Resistance Forum, All India Federation of Trade Unions, All India Nepalese Unity Society, Ankur, Bigul Mazdoor Dasta, Democratic Students Union, Delhi Pradesh Mazdoor Jan Sangathan, Disha Chhatra Sangathan, Jhuggi Jhopri Sangharsh Samiti, Mehnatkash Mazdoor Morcha, mazdoor Ekta Committee, People's Front, Progressive Students Union, Progressive Mazdoor Trade Union, Rahul Foundation, Sandhan, Saheli, Trade Union Committee of India, Workers' Solidarity.

Oxford Research Group

ORG is an independent British NGO funded by trusts and foundations, many of Quaker origin. For the past 19 years, the group has researched decision making on weapons of mass destruction and facilitated negotiations towards their ultimate elimination.

((Our hearts go out to those bereaved and wounded by the attacks on the United States. A wise response by governments will take into consideration that one of the prime motives for the attacks is to provoke a strong US counter reaction.

The group or groups responsible will almost certainly have prepared for this and will have dispersed assets and key personnel. From that perspective, the most desirable US response would be widespread military action, both immediate and sustained, against training, logistical and other anti-US paramilitary facilities in several countries, together with direct attacks against the Kabul and Baghdad regimes.

If the US takes any such action it will be precisely what the group(s) want - indeed the stronger the action the better, especially if it involves civilian casualties and stretches over a number of months. In the view of the perpetrators, such action will have many desired effects.

The classic cycle of violence, which ensures that wars follow wars, has roughly seven stages: atrocity, resulting shock and terror, fear and grief, anger, hatred, revenge, retaliation, resulting in a further atrocity and another cycle of violence.

If the west is civilised, its leaders will gather strength and wisdom to contain the emotions of their people at the fourth stage, preventing hatred hardening into another unstoppable cycle. Instead, the next stages can be as follows:

Gather allies, build coalition, follow the rule of law, bring perpetrators to justice.

Work with allies, maintain treaties, extend multilateral agreements, isolate terrorism.

Analyse underlying causes, understand antagonism, act to reduce root causes of antagonism. **"**

Project Underground
September 11, 2001

Project Underground is a coalition of individuals and groups who have consistently struggled for the rights of people and nature at mining sites around the world.

" Project Underground condemns and deplores the transformation of scores of human beings into weapons to kill thousands of people and terrorize millions more. We share in the sense of outrage, fear and loss that radiates out from these attacks and offer our deepest sympathy for those killed, injured and those without their loved ones tonight. The latest victims of senseless violence and terror are not alone. Through our work we have joined with those who have seen their loved ones killed, who have experienced terror in its many forms, who have seen their cities burned before their eyes, and who have seen their cultures crumble around them under the crushing weight of violence. We have stood with them, as they have demanded justice; and they have always reminded us that their position is little different than our own. As we seek out our own loved ones, as we face the terror of violence in our own cities, we are also again reminded of the truth of this statement. Today our society is awash in fear. But what is of greatest concern is those who would use that fear to inflict a new round of terror. We stand aghast at those who in the wake of today's tragedy can only speak in terms of dollars and cents. We watch as traders flee to the "security" of gold and oil and are reminded that that "security" has been purchased with the blood of communities with whom we work.

We are saddened and distraught that some would use the bloodshed today as the pretext for greater hate or for the reduction of freedom. We urge people not to direct their outrage at communities of color or at faith communities. Those who would increase the hold of racism or the power to control political dissent in the wake of this tragedy must not be afforded the opportunity to do so.

We are deeply and profoundly fearful of the impact of retaliatory military attacks and of the military escalation that results from a United

States military response. That needless suffering inflicted on civilians from the sky is morally unacceptable has never been clearer to the people of the United States of America.

Regrettably, all of these concerns are reinforced by the intimate connections between officials at the highest levels of the United States Government and the violent repression of the communities with which we work. We sincerely hope that the diverse sources of strength of the people of this land and solidarity between them can prove powerful enough to prevent our fears from being used to create yet another round of suffering. **〉〉**

A Call for Peace from Australia

〈〈 The organisations signed below wish to express their sincere sorrow for the enormous loss of life in the United States today. Our heartfelt condolences go out to the families and friends of the victims throughout the world as well as to the American people.

We condemn all acts of terrorism, whether state sanctioned or the actions of individuals or small groups, as indefensible. Today's tragic events show us that our current strategies are not effective and do not promote peace. The US with the assistance of Australia has been attempting to construct artificial walls around its nation through schemes such as the National Missile Defence proposal. It is clear that no amount of military spending could have created a preventative solution to the attacks witnessed by the world today. We call for a calm response in the face of this tragedy. The world needs to take a deep breath before taking rash and counterproductive steps in retaliation for these attacks. We call on the international community and the Australian people not to allow this atrocity to increase hatred, racial and religious intolerance. We encourage our leaders to view this as an opportunity for Australia to assist the US and the world in its search for peaceful solutions to conflicts.

We add our voices to those of colleagues around the world who recognise that true security can only be rooted in social and environmental justice. **〉〉**

The Wilderness Society, Earth Worker, Friends of Palestine, Friends of the Earth Australia, Action for Peace, Canberra Program for Peace, Rev. Ray Richmond, Wayside Chapel, Uniting Church in Australia, Australian AntiBases Campaign Coalition, Campaign for International Cooperation and Disarmament (CICD).

Forum of Indian Leftists
September 11, 2001

**" **We call on all those who deplore such acts to act now to prevent the proliferation of hatred, retribution, and war. We condemn the precipitous drive to put the world on a war footing against an as yet unconfirmed assailant–a move that can only compound the already immense human tragedy we have witnessed. We reiterate our belief that violence is not the solution to violence, nor can it provide a solution to longstanding political problems anywhere in the globe. It is of critical importance to stand united at this moment and denounce all acts of violence against civilians, whether by terrorists, the state, or our fellow civilians. A cycle of violence can only be broken if we work to create alternatives to violent retaliation. In the words of M.K. Gandhi, "An eye for an eye only makes the whole world blind."

As a group with a particular stake in working for peace and justice in India and its fellow South Asian nations, we are especially distressed by certain responses to this tragedy from within India. At a time when the world must stand together in unity and find ways toward peace and justice for all, we condemn polarizing and opportunistic statements from members of the Indian government and sections of the Indian press suggesting that certain nation-states such as India, Israel, and the USA must band together against others such as Pakistan and Afghanistan. We do not believe that advocating retribution against the scapegoat of "Islamic Fundamentalism" reflects the rational, democratic, non-violent, and tolerant values espoused by the majority of the Indian people. We call on the Indian government to respond to this calamity in a way that befits these values, and to stand firm against demands for uncritical support and abetment of acts of vengeance. As ordinary citizens, groups, and governments reflect and deliberate upon their responses to this terrible tragedy, we hope that all nations and peoples will use this opportunity to abandon the pursuit of intolerance, repression, and hatred in favor of reconciliation, solidarity, and reconstruction.

In this moment of grief and mourning, let us proclaim our commitment to working towards peace and justice everywhere in the world. **"**

South Asia Forum for Human Rights, Kathmandu

❝We the members of South Asia Forum for Human Rights express our anguish and shock over the criminal attacks against innocent people in the United States of America. We express our most sincere sympathy to the victims and families and people of the United States of America.

The manner in which these acts of violence were perpetrated by unknown actors or agencies leave no room for doubt about their utter disregard for human life. The use of civilian aircrafts full of innocent travellers as a weapon to strike at buildings housing thousands of people adds a new chapter to the book of horrors that the sickness of the human mind is capable of conceiving. The fact that these violent acts were carried out inside the United States, targeting the biggest commercial centre and the most secure military command centre, shows that today no nation, however powerful and security conscious, is safe from such attacks.

We appeal to the leaders of the world governments, particularly the west to strive for a just social and political world order which alone can remove the sense of injustice and discrimination that motivates desperate people to perpetrate such acts of violence against innocent peoples. ❞

The Coalition for Nuclear Disarmament and Peace (CNDP)

❝The Coalition for Nuclear Disarmament and Peace (CNDP) condemns the indiscriminate mass murder perpetrated in the USA on 11 September, 2001 using hijacked passenger aircraft as weapons. CNDP joins the world in expressing its heartfelt condolences to the bereaved families and the American people. There can be no justification for mass murder committed either by stateless fanatical groups or by states. This is the reason that the peace movement, all over the world, opposes weapons of mass destruction such as nuclear, biological and chemical weapons. September 11 has shown that mass murder today does not need sophisticated technology. Such barbaric activity poisons all peace processes, and sets back all efforts at disarmament. This crime also shows that neither nuclear weapons nor defence shields (NMD/TMD) provide any additional 'security'.

There will be forces in the United States government and elsewhere calling for retaliatory strikes and reprisals. Any response that does not distinguish between perpetrators and innocent people will be no different from the barbaric acts of 11th September that have drawn justified worldwide condemnation. It is also necessary to distinguish between the acts of terrorism and the causes driving it. Addressing only terrorist acts will not stop the current spiral of violence. Negotiated and just settlements of various conflicts around the world are the only long term guarantees for peace and against terrorism.

It appears that the United States, is now preparing for unilateral action in Afghanistan. CNDP strongly believes that any such action should only be under the aegis of the UN. CNDP believes that India should not be a party to such unilateral US action and, deplores the Vajpayee government's willingness to compromise India's sovereignty. **"**

Coalition for an International Criminal Court

" On behalf of the more than 1000 members of the NGO Coalition for the International Criminal Court, we wish to express our horror and shock over the criminal attacks perpetrated yesterday against innocent people in the USA.

We express our most sincere sympathy to the victims, their families and the people of the United States of America. We are also thinking of the many people affected every day by terrorism, genocide, crimes against humanity and other atrocities in all parts of the world.

This horrific crime clearly demonstrates the need for a fundamentally strengthened system of international criminal justice. The International Criminal Court is expected to be established in 2002-2003 after entry into force of the Rome Statute of the ICC. It will be permanent and independent and will prosecute individuals who commit genocide, war crimes, and crimes against humanity.

Though the international community has not been able to agree on the definition of the crime of international terrorism, it is our unanimous opinion that yesterday's acts of terrorism were crimes against humanity the murder of hundreds if not thousands of innocent civilians.

We appeal to the government of the US and its allies to focus on bringing the perpetrators to justice and warn against indiscriminate military retaliation. Such retaliation has been the response to past terrorist attacks - it is not only illegal but has been ineffective and will inevitably result in more deaths and a cycle of recrimination, revenge and terrorism. This cannot be the response of a civilized nation hoping to put an end to this kind of violence.

The world community must join together in condemning this terrorist crime against humanity and join in using national and international laws in bringing those responsible to justice. 〞

Human Rights Watch

〝We profoundly condemn yesterday's cruel attacks in the United States and express our condolences to the victims and This was an assault not merely on one nation or one people, but on principles of respect for civilian life cherished by all We urge all governments to unite to investigate this crime, to prevent its recurrence, and to bring to justice those who are responsible.

Last night, President Bush said that the United States "will make no distinction between the terrorists who committed these acts and those who shelter them. Yet distinctions must be made: between the guilty and the innocent; between the perpetrators and the civilians who may surround them; between those who commit atrocities and those who may simply share their religious beliefs, ethnicity or national origin. People committed to justice and law and human rights must never descend to the level of the perpetrators. That is the most important distinction of all. 〞

Condemning Terrorist Attacks
September 17, 2001

〝The terrorist outrage against innocent men, women and children in various US cities on 11 September 2001 is feared to have claimed several thousand lives and inflicted injuries to even more people. Crimes against innocent people are crimes against all humanity and the perpetrators of these grotesque crimes should be brought to justice. At the same time, it is important that the Government of the United States does not fall prey to the same sort of perverted psychology that drives fanatics to perpetuate terrorist acts against innocent people. Military retaliation and revenge can result in grievous injury to innocent lives in areas suspected of harbouring suspects. Just as civilized governments are not deterred by dastardly acts of terror similarly victims of indiscriminate revenge attacks cannot accept that they should be punished for crimes they have not committed. It is therefore important that no action is taken without proper investigation and identification of the culprits. It is imperative that the terrorists involved in the present crime and others all over the world are denied safe haven everywhere, and the whole world community works together to exclude and isolate such barbarians and they are brought to justice. In the longer run one has to consider in a rational and dispassionate manner what drives people to such acts of utter desperation. Unless those causes are removed the spectre of violence will continue to loom large over the horizons the world over. Therefore it is important that justice is provided to all. It is now, more than ever before, necessary to examine seriously the non-violent alternative provided by Mahatma Gandhi and effectively employed by Dr Martin Luther King Jr. and other leaders of the world to challenge and defeat forces representing brute might.

Ishtiaq Ahmed, Ajaz Anwar, Hassan Gardezi, Harsh Kapoor, Asghar Ali Engineer, Pervez Hoodbhoy, Michele Micheletti, Anil Viakara, Rafi Khawaja, Gulzar Ahmed, Bilal Hashmi, Cecil Chaudhry, Ameek A. Ponda, Leo Rebello, Partha S. Ghosh, Kripa Sundar, Sharmila Gopinathan, Pritam Singh, J. Sri Raman, Razia Malik, Robin Khundkar, Pritam K. Rohila, Keizer Mustafa Hussain, Kaushik Thakrar, Colonel Brian Cloughley, Susan M. Akram, Ilyas Khan, Sain Sucha, Babar Mumtaz, Björn Beckman, Henrik Berglund, Ghazala Anwar, Geoffrey Cook, Abul Fazal Mahmud, SM & Asha Shahed, Syeda Khundkar, Zafar Iqbal, Nuzaira Azam, Fr. Joe Mangalam, Sukla Sen, A.H. Nayyar, T.N. Gopalan, Ammu Abraham, Khalid Lakhani, R. Arul, Pasumai Thaayagam, Yahya Hassan Bajwa, Khalid Duran, Paul Wallace, Prakash N. Shah, Ajay K. Mehra, Pramod Kumar, Inayatullah, Welay Songur, Riaz Cheema, Vikram Vyas, Satish Saberwal, Khushi Muhammad Khan, Magnus Lembke

Jagori Sangat
September 14, 2001

“ We, 240 participants of the Jagori Sangat (South Asian Network of Gender Activists and Trainers)/Jagori workshop "Surviving Crises, Rebuilding Resistance: Women's Struggles for Sustainable Development" being held in Kathmandu, are shocked at the recent incident of violence in the USA, with the loss of many innocent lives. Such violence can never be justified; no matter what the cause that inspires it.

As representatives of women's groups and people's movements in Nepal, Pakistan, Sri Lanka, Bangladesh and India, we are also deeply concerned about the possibility of retaliatory violence on a global scale. We believe that violence will only breed further violence and create large-scale devastation the world over.

We also wish to make it clear that the expression of solidarity in the cause of fighting the problem of "international terrorism" does not in any way condone the daily crimes perpetrated on the rest of the world by the US government and American corporations, using every kind of economic, military and intellectual weapon.

Our lives, our rights and our futures are being threatened by the increasing acceptance of violence as a means of political expression and dispute resolution. We are raising our voices against the breakdown of democratic dialogue and collective processes of consensus building in many of our countries. We can no longer expend our energies on the destructive enterprise of war – this is our last chance to begin the search for a solution to these seemingly intractable issues in a manner that upholds democratic rights of all sections of the society and ensures that our right to live in peace and dignity are not violated. 〃

Diverse Women for Diversity
October 1, 2001

Signed by 40 women from the five continents of the world, in New Delhi.

❝ We, women of diversity committed to a peaceful world, celebrate our differences. From our differences come our strengths. We come from all the continents, different faiths, cultures and races and are united in our vision for peace and justice for the world today. We want to leave a more peaceful and just world for our children and for the generations to come. We celebrate and uphold cultural diversity. we will defend all forms of diversity and resist all forms of monoculture, fundamentalism and violence from which intolerance and hatred arise.

The tragedy on September 11 has shown us another face of terror.

We join in the pain of all people who have faced the terror of those who do not value the sanctity of human life. We especially abhor the use of human beings themselves as weapons. In this regard the terror of September 11 cannot be viewed as a lone event. Many acts of this such terror have been inflicted on the peoples of this earth. The sacredness and dignity of human life and the right to peaceful existence and justice have been destroyed through the fundamentalism of imperialistic globalisation and religious fundamentalism.

Among the many tools of terror in the modern world are:

- economic sanctions that lead to starvation and disease epidemics;
- biotechnologies that threaten the roots of life;
- monocultures that destroy social and biological diversity;

- degradation of the environment for monetary gain;
- widespread application of pesticides that lead to deformities and death;
- pollution of soils, water and ecosystems at large;
- the pursuit of profit by global corporations at the expense of sustainable livelihoods, cultural identities, and the right of people to basic necessities of life, including corporate monopolies on water, seeds, food and medicine;
- patriarchy, racism, casteism which negates and violate the majority of the world.

Given the extent of such structural terror in the world it is perhaps surprising that direct terrorist attacks, like that of September 11, are not more common. If we want to end terrorism we must pay attention to all sources of injustice that widen the gap between rich and poor, men and women, nature and humans and create the hopelessness that can lead to terrorism. We stand with those who are working to remove the structural causes of injustices.

Women, children, the differently-abled and the aged are the worst victims of this reign of terror:

- the terror of not having water to drink and food to eat;
- the terror of food and water contamination;
- the terror of losing home, homeland, family and community and becoming a refugee;
- the terror of persistent poverty that leads to the sale of life and body organs;
- the terror of being forced into prostitution as means of survival;
- the terror of living in communities where drug abuse has become a way of life;
- the terror of losing our children to a culture of violence and to all kinds of conflicts and wars;
- the terror of domestic and other violence against girls and women;
- the terror of living in a society where basic human rights for women are not respected;

We women of diversity pledge ourselves to work against terrorism in all its forms and to work positively towards a world free of war, hunger and social and economic injustices. We condemn all acts of war and call on all nations to boycott pacts of aggression. We invite all women of the world to join with us in stopping governments from rushing into a mindless global war. Together, we will find peaceful, creative and non violent ways to end terrorism in all its forms.

We ask all people of the world to stand with us in defending and celebrating diversity, peace and hope. **"**

Candle-Light Vigil for Restraint & Peace
India Gate, New Delhi
September 19, 2001

" We, as Indian citizens and as people of good conscience, committed to peace and justice, record our shock and sorrow at the death and destruction caused by the 11 September 2001 attacks on the United States, and express our sincere sympathy to the ordinary citizens who have suffered loss and bereavement

The use of such violence cannot be justified, no matter what the cause that inspires it. But neither can the use of retaliatory violence and armed force be justified. We condemn the outpouring of hatred and the calls for war and armed reprisal, and the deployment of forces, that have followed the attack.

While we, like millions of others, want the spiral of violence to stop, and stand against terrorism of all kinds, we are equally concerned about the mounting movement towards a "new war." We are shocked to see and hear the language of war and hatred being used by the United States and many other governments. Preparations are being made for all-out war against nations and religious groups even before anyone knows conclusively who was behind the attacks on the United States.

This can be achieved and secured only if we can rise to genuine humanity and statesmanship at an hour such as this. We must search for solutions to these seemingly intractable issues in a manner that upholds the rights of all, and ensures that the right of all people to live in peace and dignity are not violated. We believe that violence will only breed further violence and lead to large-scale devastation the world over.

We call on all governments, including our own, to exercise caution and to counsel against the kind of unrestrained official reaction we are seeing now. Hate attacks and the killing of innocent people in the US and Britain have already begun. We know that both warfare and hatred could reach a scale of unforeseeable proportions. We ask all our governments to work for genuine international coexistence and peace, and not to become party to measures by any government or alliance seeking to promote its own military interests or pursue its own policy agendas in any region in the name of fighting terrorism.

We stand together against the menace of retaliatory violence. **"**

Action India, AIDWA, Akhil Bharat Rachnatmak Samaj, All Asia Peace Foundation, Ankur, Anuradha Chenoy, Association of Peoples of Asia, Bindia Thapar, Brinda Singh, CWDS, Dev Chopra, FORCES, Guild of Service, HAQ Centre for Child Rights, Indian Social Action Forum (INSAF), Indian Social Institute, Jagori, Joint Women's Programme, Kali for Women, Kamal Chenoy, Labour File, Lawyers' Collective, Lokayan, Mahila Chetna Kendra, Mohamed Bashir Abbasi, Muslim Women's Forum, NAFRE, National Federation of Indian Women, Nirantar, Nirmala Deshpande, Nishant Natya Manch, North East Network, Pakistan-India People's Forum for Peace and Democracy, PEACE, Radical Humanist Association, Razia Ismail Abbasi, SAHMAT, Sanjiv Kaura, South Asian Network of Gender Activists and Trainers (SANGAT), Sushoba Barve, Women's Coalition for Peace and Development with Dignity, Women's Initiative for Peace in South Asia (WIPSA), YWCA of India

Indian Women Against War

❝We are women from different autonomous women's groups, NGOs, development organizations, academia, and individual women. We come from different states, cities or villages, having different political persuasions, belonging to various cultures, from different class, caste and religious backgrounds, and speaking diverse languages. We are bound together by a vision that upholds equality, gender-justice, peace and democracy. For decades now we have been engaged in multi-faceted struggles that aim to bring about a world where every individual has the right to life with dignity and equality.

It is with great shock and horror that we have witnessed the developments that have unfolded the world over since the attacks on the US on 11th Sept 2001. We condemn the loss of innocent lives and offer our sympathies to those bereaved in this tragedy.

Yet, we note with regret that this recent act of violence is one that has had many precedents all over the world: Hiroshima and Nagasaki, Iran, Iraq, Bosnia, South Africa to name only a few. In this context the US has been a major world player and cannot absolve itself of direct responsibility for acts and policies that have brought the death of thousands in other parts of the world. If terrorism is to be blamed for the WTC attacks then the US would have to recognise the role it has played in nurturing the very terrorists that it seeks to bring to book today.

One way or another we have all been part of these violent histories: as witnesses, as those affected, as pawns in the hands of leaders, as citizens, as women. In the past, we have continued with our struggle to create a world that respects human life and dignity. We have continued to hope that there will be new beginnings: in big and small ways we have moved forward. We have dared to hope in the midst of all the hatred, all the anger.

Today, all of this is threatened. Our work, our struggles, our visions, our hopes. There is nothing heroic about war; this "new war" or the ones waged in the past. We have seen the aftermath of war and related crimes; thousands of women have lived through the burden of bearing the ‘honour’ of community and nation in war after war. Bruised minds, battered bodies: that is all that war will achieve. We know this, just as surely as we know that our futures are threatened by any possible war now.

We therefore urge all national leaders and politicians to refrain from taking any steps that will jeopardise peace and democracy in South Asia and the rest of the world. We urge extreme caution and wisdom in formulating strategies to tackle the present situation. Such a situation could also be turned into an opportunity for dialogue by informed leadership. All relevant issues must be addressed with due recourse to democratic norms and non-violent dialogue. We believe that armed conflict can never be, and never has been a substitute for dialogue. Failure to pursue democratic dialogue is to betray the aspirations of millions, to jeopardise the future and to put into question the very existence of democratic institutions and mechanisms.

This is not our war. We reject it unequivocally. We stand together in our opposition to war with others: with peace groups, people's movements, civil liberties organisations, students groups, environment groups, and ordinary women, men and children. We do not believe in this war for it snatches away from us one of the most basic rights: the right to life. **"**

Gujarat Forum of Women's Studies and Action Groups, Gujarat, Sahiyar, Vadodara, Olakh, Vadodara, Jagori, Delhi, Saheli, Delhi, Forum Against Oppression of Women, Mumbai, Arundhati Roy, Delhi, Nandini Manjrekar, Vadodara, Bina Srinivasan, Vadodara, Bhavana Mehta, Vadodara, Neeraben Desai, Mumbai, Sophia Khan, Ahmedabad, Shiney Verghese, Vadodara, Viraj Pandit, Ahmedabad, Sonal Mehta, Ahmedabad, Chirashree Thakkar, Ahmedabad, Subha De, Vadodara, Nilima Shiekh, Vadodara, Hina Desai, Ahmedabad, Nandini Oza, Badwani, Medha Patkar, Mumbai, Chittaroopa Palit, Maheshwar, Akshara, Mumbai, Richa Nagar, Lucknow, Deeksha Nagar, Lucknow, Malini Subramanian, Bhopal, Rekha Rodwittiya, Vadodara, Shashi Mehta, Mumbai, Manjula Ramanan, Vadodara,Deeptha Achar, Vadodara, Gargi Rargiraina, Vadodara, Purvi Vyas, Ahmedabad.

Global Vigil for Peace on October 2, 2001

❝ On September 17, many of us who had gathered at the India Gate lawns decided to give a call to people around the world to organise peace vigils in October 2, the birth anniversary of Gandhi. The invitation to organise this Global Peace Vigil said; "While we use names like Gandhi and King, we also remember all those from Buddha and Jesus to Prophet Mohammed, along with all those women and men who worked for peace, tolerance, compassion and sharing in different parts of the world. October 2 was selected because it provides a convenient date around which to build on the proven abilities of persons like Gandhi to convince millions representing diverse beliefs and opinions, of the critical need for tolerance, equity and justice as critical ingredients for peace – and above all that the struggle to achieve these must be non-violent, because the means were as important as the ends.

"Co-ordinating action around the world on a particular date might also help achieve that important ingredient – a critical mass and hopefully a chain reaction of good impulses which indeed is the only way to achieve operation INFINITE JUSTICE!"

Vigils were held in over 40 countries. In Delhi, about 300 of us gathered next to Gandhi's resting place. We sang songs and pledged to coomit ourselves to the struggle for sanity and peace. **❞**

Illustration by Bindia Thapar